MAKING

50 *Illuminating Projects,Techniques & Ideas*

GREAT
LAMPS

KYLE SPENCER
Dice Light
8"x 8"x 8"

MAKING

50 *Illuminating Projects, Techniques & Ideas*

GREAT
LAMPS

Deborah Morgenthal

LARK
BOOKS

To my daughter Corrina,
the light of my life

Art Director: Dana Irwin

Production: Dana Irwin and Hannes Charen

Photography: Richard Babb

Illustrations: Olivier Rollin

Library of Congress Cataloging-in-Publication Data
Morgenthal, Deborah, 1950-

    Making great lamps : 50 illuminating projects, techniques, and ideas   / Deborah Morgenthal. -- 1st ed.
    p. cm.
    Includes index.
    ISBN 1-57990-057-7 (hard)
    1. Lamps. 2. Lampshades. I. Title.
TT897.2.M67 1998   98-21475
749'.63--dc21   CIP

10 9 8 7 6 5 4 3 2 1

First Edition

Published by Lark Books
50 College St.
Asheville, NC 28801, US

© 1998, Lark Books

Distributed by Random House, Inc., in the United States, Canada, the United Kingdom, Europe,and Asia
Distributed in Australia by Capricorn Link (Australia) Pty Ltd., P.O. Box 6651, Baulkham Hills Business Centre, NSW 2153, Australia
Distributed in New Zealand by Tandem Press Ltd., 2 Rugby Rd., Birkenhead, Auckland, New Zealand

Printed in Hong Kong
All rights reserved
ISBN 1-57990-057-7

Contents

MAKING GREAT LAMPS

oths are not the only creatures drawn to light. People are very affected by light—sunlight, moonlight, and lamp light. Fortunately for those of us who feel a particular passion about the latter, the attraction is not a fatal one! In fact, the popularity of lamps has resulted in an incandescent explosion of possibilities. Many home furnishing stores carry dozens of lighting options, ranging from traditional to contemporary. This allows buyers to creatively illuminate every room in their home, and, simultaneously, make a design statement that reflects their individual taste.

■

The only bad news is that most of the truly inspiring lamps found in shops are very expensive. That's why we put this book together. We invited 22 talented designers to create lamps they'd like to live with, and the result is a collection of 60 exciting and diverse do-it-yourself projects. You'll find many different types of lamps—floor lamps, chandeliers, night lights, sconces, and table lamps—made from paper, wood, metal, and other traditional as well as unusual materials, reflecting a remarkable range of styles and moods.

The projects are organized into three sections: Making Lamps from Common Objects, Transforming the Old and Ordinary, and Making Lamps from Traditional and Uncommon Materials.

You can make a lamp from nearly any kind of object, from a favorite wooden toy to a classy vintage shoe. The book features 18 projects that electrify a variety of objects, including a bird cage, a metal gear, and a stack of books. Each project encourages you to look at the world of objects around you in a new light.

Another way to create imaginative lighting is to give an old or plain lamp a makeover. The book includes 15 projects that turn the ordinary into the extraordinary. This section may inspire you to look at the lamps in your home and see ways to really turn them on (sorry. . . it's so hard to resist all the—illuminating—expressions).

Lastly, the book offers 27 fantastic lamps you can make from scratch, using a variety of materials and craft techniques, including paper mache, wood, handmade paper, beading, and decorative painting. This sec-

tion truly demonstrates that interesting lighting can be an integral, even a focal point, in home decorating.

The book describes in detail how to electrify an object, using lamp parts available from home centers, hardware stores, and mail-order catalogs. Many of these outlets offer lamp kits made specifically for wiring different types of objects. Even for people wary of electricity, it's not at all scary to turn a colander into a lamp. If you're really worried about the process, you can have a lamp shop electrify the object for you. In addition, the book provides instructions for making a basic lamp shade, and offers suggestions for matching shade styles to bases of particular shapes.

Thanks to the talent and enthusiasm of the designers, this book glows with the lumens of a 150-watt bulb! We're certain you'll find many projects you'll want to make and many ideas that will inspire you to make unique lamps that reflect your love of light and lighting.

HOW TO ASSEMBLE AND WIRE A LAMP

Many of the projects in this book require that you electrify a lamp. You can take your Aunt Selma's vase, a miniature sailboat, or a carburetor part to a lamp shop that specializes in making lamps, pick out a shade, and let the store staff assemble and wire the lamp for you. Or, with the information provided in this book, you can wire the lamp yourself.

The two lamps on page 9 were made by Diane Weaver.

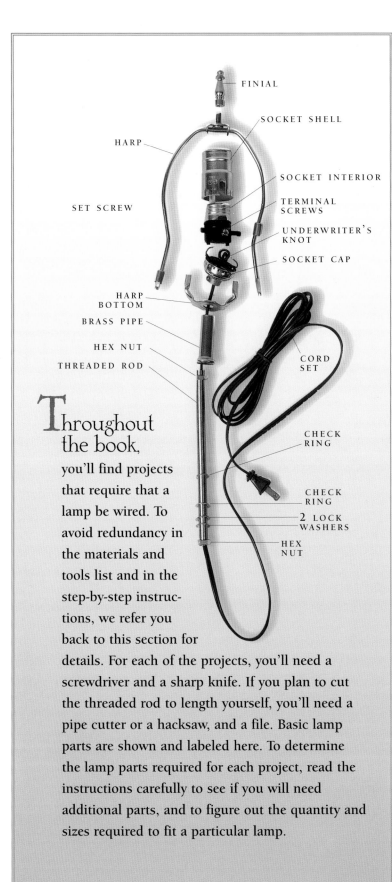

FINIAL

SOCKET SHELL

HARP

SET SCREW

SOCKET INTERIOR

TERMINAL SCREWS

UNDERWRITER'S KNOT

SOCKET CAP

HARP BOTTOM

BRASS PIPE

HEX NUT

THREADED ROD

CORD SET

CHECK RING

CHECK RING

2 LOCK WASHERS

HEX NUT

Throughout the book, you'll find projects that require that a lamp be wired. To avoid redundancy in the materials and tools list and in the step-by-step instructions, we refer you back to this section for details. For each of the projects, you'll need a screwdriver and a sharp knife. If you plan to cut the threaded rod to length yourself, you'll need a pipe cutter or a hacksaw, and a file. Basic lamp parts are shown and labeled here. To determine the lamp parts required for each project, read the instructions carefully to see if you will need additional parts, and to figure out the quantity and sizes required to fit a particular lamp.

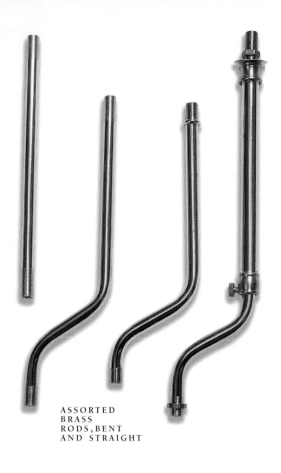

ASSORTED
BRASS
RODS, BENT
AND STRAIGHT

LINE
SWITCHES,
CANDLE
SOCKETS,
AND LAMP
CORDS

SOCKET
SHELL

SOCKET
INTERIOR

SOCKET
CAP

LOCK
WASHER

HARP
BOTTOM

CHECK
RING

HEX NUT

WASHER

RUBBER
PLUG

NIPPLE

LOCK
WASHER

HEX NUT

BOTTLE
LAMP
KIT

The photographs on pages 22 to 23 are intended to inspire you to make lamps from—well, almost anything! But as the project here demonstrates, there is nothing mysterious about wiring a lamp yourself. So why not grab that beloved cowboy boot or stuffed toy monkey and give it a try?

Most hardware stores, home centers, lamp shops, as well as specialized mail-order catalogs (see the Supplier List on page 142) carry the lamp components required for the job, including threaded rods in many lengths and widths, and lock washers, check rings, and nuts sized to match. The photographs on pages 9-10 and 18 identify a variety of the lamp parts. You can purchase these parts individually or as part of a lamp kit. These kits come with very good instructions, so be sure to read them thoroughly.

The following project describes how to assemble and wire a lamp from a hardwood board, a few weathered wooden columns, and a good-looking shade. If, after reading the instructions, you're still uneasy about the wiring process, take your lamp to a lamp shop and let their trained staff electrify it for you.

Dana's Lamp

Art director Dana Irwin loved these old wooden columns and knew one day she would find a way to bring their beauty to light.

What You Need

piece of wood for base
object that can be drilled through
quick-dry lacquer spray paint, black or color of your choice
lamp parts, including $\frac{3}{8}$-inch (9 mm)
threaded rod, 1-inch washer (2.5 cm) with matching check rings, lock washers, nipple, nuts, hex nuts, prelacquered brass pipe, socket base, push-socket, cross bar, 16- or 18-gauge stranded lamp wire, plug, harp and harp bottom, finial
wood screws, 2½ inches (6 cm) long
white craft glue
felt
light bulb
measuring tools
saw
router
drill with assorted bits
sander or sandpaper
pipe cutter
hacksaw
file
pliers
needle-nose pliers
screwdriver
sharp knife

What You Do

1. Measure and cut the base (see photos 2 and 3). Sand the wood.

2. Rout the base (sees photo 4 and 5). Always cut against the grain first so the sides won't split.

3. Mark the center point of the base (see photo 6). Drill a ¼-inch (6 mm) pilot hole in the center (see photo 7). Then drill a second ¼-inch (6 mm) pilot hole in the side of the base for the wire to pass through (photo 8).

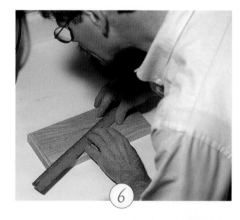

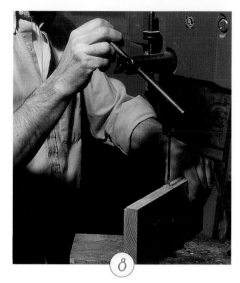

4. Change to a 1⅛-inch (3.6 cm) bit and turn the base over. Drill out the center hole three-fourths of the way through the board (photos 9 and 10).

5. Switch to a ⅞16-inch bit and drill through the board on the top side (see photo 11). Sand the board well.

6. Spray the base with the black lacquer and let dry (see photo 12). Apply three coats, letting each coat dry thoroughly.

7. Trim the bottoms of the wooden columns. Choose the column that will be in the center of the lamp, and drill a ⅞16-inch hole all the way through (see photo 13). Use a drill bit that is longer than the piece you're drilling. Turn the column over and keep drilling until you have drilled through the piece (see photo 14).

8. Photo 15 shows some of the lamp parts you will need.

9. Slip the 1-inch (2.5 cm) washer onto the threaded rod, and tighten with a lock washer and nut (see photo 16 on page 14.)

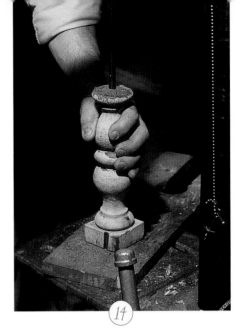

10. Attach the side columns to the base by countersinking 2½ inch-long (6 cm) screws through the bottom of the base and into the columns. Insert the threaded rod through the bottom of the base (see photo 17 on page 14); the washers and nut are locked in place in the hole on the bottom of the base.

11. The brass pipe (the lamp neck) will slip over the threaded rod and sit flush against the top of the center column and will lift the shade away from the columns at a pleasing height. Measure a 2-inch (5 cm) section on

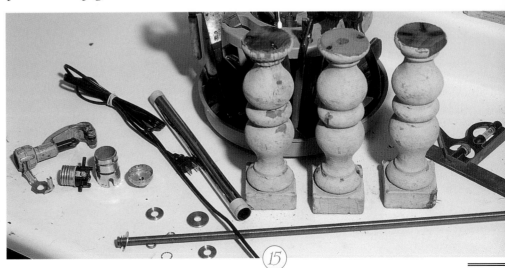

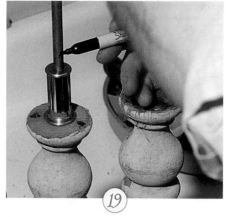

the pipe and mask it where you will be cutting so you don't scratch the lacquer coating. Cut the pipe gradually, making several cuts to prevent crushing the pipe. Tighten the tension of the cutter as you make each cut (see photo 18).

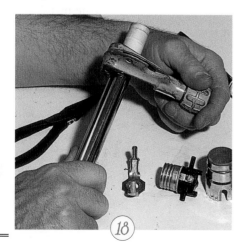

12. Slip the brass pipe onto the threaded rod. Mark the threaded rod ¾ inch (2 cm) above the brass pipe (see photo 19). Remove the brass pipe and cut the threaded rod with a hack saw or pipe cutter.

13. Use the pliers to pull up the threaded rod. Insert the needle-nose pliers into the threaded rod and ream out the inside sharp edges so the lamp wire won't be damaged (see photo 20).

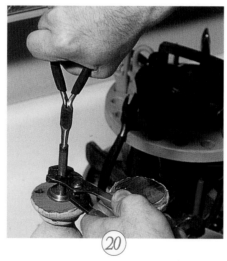

14. Stack the two check rings on the rod, with the large one facing up and the small one facing down (see photo 21). Then slip on the brass pipe and another nut (see photo 22). Slip on another check ring and then a hex nut on top (see photo 23); tighten.

15. Add the harp bottom (see photo 24) and screw the socket base as snugly as possible over the protruding threaded rod (see photos 25 and 26). Tighten the socket base set screw.

16. Insert the lamp wire through the hole in the side of the base and then through the hole in the bottom of the base (see photo 27). Pull out more wire than you need so you have plenty to work with. Slip the wire up through the threaded rod and out the socket base at the top (see photo 28).

17. Split the wire and make an Underwriters' Knot (see photos 28 and 29) and pull tight.

(24)

(27)

(30)

(25)

the wires inside the socket. Always connect the lead (ribbed or with color tracer or white strands) to the white terminal screw. If you follow these instructions correctly, you will maintain the polarity of a correctly wired system.

19. Slide the metal socket shell (with insulating liner inside) over the socket so the switch (if any) is seated in the slots (see photo 30). Push the shell firmly into the socket until it locks

(26)

(28)

(31)

(29)

18. Strip the end of each wire to expose ½ inch (1.5 cm) of bare copper strands, being careful not to damage the wire strands or the insulation beyond the stripped length. Twist the copper strands of each wire tightly together, loop each wire clockwise three-quarters of a turn around the proper terminal screw, and tighten the screw securely over the loop. Pay very close attention to how you connect

securely and evenly in position. To assure locking, push on the metal shell only.

20. Attach the plug to the other end of the wire, being sure to attach the ground wire to the aluminum screw.

21. Cover the threaded rod with a bent, solid brass pole (see photo 31).

22. Glue felt to the bottom of the base.

23. Attach the harp. Screw in the light bulb.

24. Attach the shade and finial.

Light Bulbs

Light bulbs are available in a wide range of sizes, shapes, and strengths to match a variety of needs and lamp styles. Light bulbs differ most dramatically from one another in terms of their quality of light. Scales are used to assess the color temperature the bulb gives off and how the light from that bulb affects the objects it's lighting. The term Correlated Color Temperature (CCT) is used to compare the warmth or coolness of light as it's produced. Bulbs are rated according to the Kelvin (K) temperature scale. The blue of the sky is near the top of the scale at 10,000K, whereas the glow of candlelight is about 1,000K. Color Rendition Index (CRI) describes how a light source affects the sense of the colors of objects it illuminates, such as furniture or flesh tones. The index ranges from 1 to 100, with 100 being closest to how an object looks in sunlight. Experiment with bulbs with similar CCT but with different CRIs and see what looks you can achieve.

The most commonly used and least expensive bulbs are the *incandescents*. Their soft, warm glow is similar to candlelight. However, they are the least efficient; about 90 percent of their electricity goes into heat generation, rather than light production. The bulb converts electric power into light by passing electric current through a filament of tungsten wire. The wire consists of minicoils that are coiled into larger coils. The current heats the tungsten filament until it glows. The high melting temperature slows the filament's evaporation; to further slow it, the bulb is usually filled with an inert gas mixture.

Halogen bulbs, although basically an incandescent, have a few traits that make them superi-

or. They are far more energy efficient, and although more expensive, they usually pay for themselves over the life of the bulb. Halogens also produce light when electricity heats a tungsten filament. The difference is that the halogen gas in the bulb causes particles of tungsten to be redeposited onto the tungsten filament. The result is that the lamp lasts longer and is whiter and brighter throughout its life.

Fluorescent lamps are based on a completely different technology. They are glass tubes coated on the interior with phosphor, a chemical compound that emits light when activated by ultraviolet energy. Air in the tubes is replaced with argon gas and a small amount of mercury is added. When a fluorescent lamp is turned on, the electricity heats cathodes at each end, causing them to emit electrons, which then create an electric arc between the cathodes. The electrons in this arc collide with mercury vapor and argo to produce invisible ultraviolet rays, which excite the fluorescent phosphor coating, producing visible light. These bulbs are extremely energy efficient, and are available in a variety of shapes. Compact fluorescent bulbs are another option, and have the advantage of screwing into bases just like incandescent bulbs.

Technology is improving bulbs. New bulbs are available that dim or shut themselves off, encourage plant growth, or are shatter-proof. You can find a wide range of decorative bulbs—clear and frosted—to use in chandeliers, sconces, fan lights, vanity lights, and traditional fixtures. The type of light you select can alter the look of a lamp and create distinctive lighting effects.

LAMP SHADE BASICS

Thanks to the ready availability of lamp shade frames and parts, and the extraordinary range of papers, fabrics, and finials to choose from, now you can make lamp shades to match your every mood and home-decor.

The basics of lamp shade construction are simple: You adhere shade material to a frame. Then you connect the shade to a harp that is attached to the lamp socket, or you set the frame directly onto the light bulb, using a top ring that comes with a special clasp.

Most of the projects in this book use purchased lamp shades. But others require that you make the shade, either by starting from scratch or by adhering new paper or fabric to a lamp shade frame. You can also put a new shade on an old wire frame; simply remove the old covering and sand off any remaining adhesive.

There are many, many shapes and styles of ready-made shades on the market. Selecting the right shade for a base can be challenging. The chart on page 21 pairs different shaped bases with various shade styles to help you choose the perfect shade.

If you are making a *shade from scratch,* here are some important guidelines.

■ Unless you are using a catalog with photographs or drawings of supplies, always bring the lamp base with you to the fabric or paper-supply store.

■ Hold potential papers or fabrics up to the light to see how their color and texture are affected by light shining through them.

■ If you are mail-ordering, ask for or purchase samples.

■ Before you purchase your covering material, write down all the required measurements and take them along to the store (along with a calculator) so you can be sure to buy the correct amount. When in doubt, buy a little extra.

■ Keep in mind that fabrics can be stiffened with a layer of styrene (an adhesive plastic with a peel-away backing) or with a fusible knit interfacing. Lamp shade-supply companies offer a wide and attractive selection of prelaminated fabrics. Almost every type of decorative paper can be used, although many require a low-watt bulb and are not colorfast and will fade if exposed to direct sunlight. There are also heavier papers designed just for lamp shade making.

■ Decide what type of fitter wire you will use to attach the shade to the lamp (clip top, clip-on bulb, washer top, chimney top, etc.)

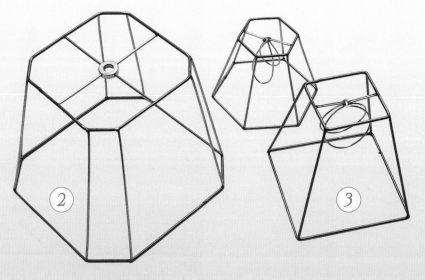

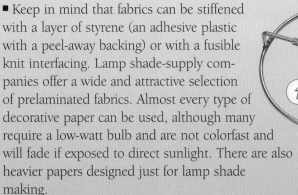

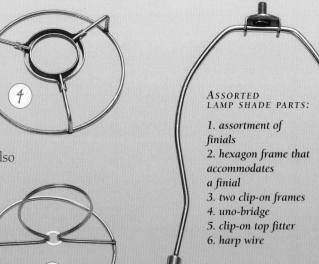

ASSORTED
LAMP SHADE PARTS:

1. *assortment of finials*
2. *hexagon frame that accommodates a finial*
3. *two clip-on frames*
4. *uno-bridge*
5. *clip-on top fitter*
6. *harp wire*

18

Making a Cone-Shaped Shade

One of the most popular lamp shade shapes is the cone. This project walks you through the basic steps of making this type of shade.

What You Need

top lamp shade ring
bottom lamp shade ring
predrafted arc pattern OR piece of 65- to 80-pound cover-weight paper
pencil
fabric or paper for the shade
⅝-inch (1.6-cm) grosgrain cotton ribbon trim
bulldog clips
measuring tape
weights
white craft glue
wax paper
scissors
craft knife
drafting compass

What You Do

1. Measure the diameter of the top and bottom rings, and determine how tall you want your shade to be. Use these three measurements to purchase a predrafted arc pattern. Or, you can copy the arc from an old shade, if the dimensions match. A well-drafted arc pattern will fall perfectly onto the rings. If it doesn't, don't trim off the excess material or you will change the dimensions and wind up with a lop-sided shade.

2. Mark the center front of your arc pattern at the top and bottom, adding a ½-inch (1.5 cm) back seam allowance on the right edge. Place the arc pattern on the wrong side of your paper or fabric, and add weights at both edges to prevent shifting. Trace the outline with a pencil, then mark the center and a ¼-inch (6 mm) seam allowance on the arc you have cut from the shade material.

3. Hold the bottom wire ring in line with your body with one hand. Hold the bottom center front of the arc on the wire ring and fasten the edge of the shade material with a bulldog clip (see figure 1). Alternating work between the left and the right sides, continue fitting and fastening the arc to the ring, using a generous number of clips until you reach the end of the arc (see figure 2).

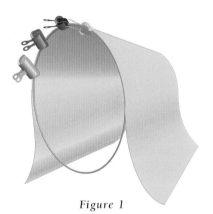

Figure 1

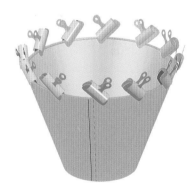

Figure 2

4. Return to the center front and fit the right half to the ring. When you reach the end, overlap the back seam, left over right, and fasten with a bull-dog clip. Make sure the arc has no gaps and that the arc's edge fits evenly around the edge. Fit the top ring to the arc in the same manner. Check the top and the bottom for a smooth, snug fit (see figure 3 on page 20).

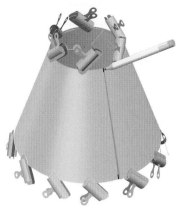

Figure 3

Figure 5

8. Finish the top and bottom edges with decorative trim; ⅞-inch (1.6 cm) grosgrain ribbon is the most popular binding, but colored tapes, velvets, and twills work well, too. Avoid polyester trims as they don't stretch well or bond well with glue. To figure out how much binding to purchase, multiply the top and bottom ring diameters by four and then add them together.

5. With the back seam facing you, lightly mark the top and bottom seam allowance. Remove all the clips and set the rings aside. Place the arc on a flat surface with its right side facing up. Connect the top and bottom markings and trim off any excess material. Turn the arc over so its right side faces up. Apply a line of glue along the entire length of both sides of the back seam overlap (see figure 4).

Figure 6

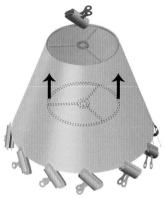

Figure 8

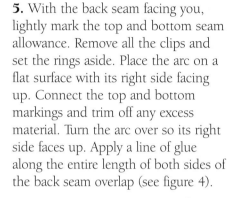

Figure 4

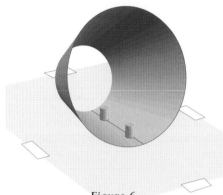

Figure 7

9. Use a drafting compass to draw a guideline around the top and bottom edges (see figure 9). When working on the bottom edge, allow a portion of the shade to hang over the edge. Square off one end of the binding for the top of the shade (see figure 10). Apply glue to the lower half of the first few inches, starting at the squared off end. Working from the back seam, position the binding ¼ inch (6 mm) to the left of the seam overlap. Finger-press the trim into place and let dry.

6. Line up the top right edge of the arc with the left side's pencil mark and fasten with a bulldog clip placed perpendicular to the arc's edge (figure 5). Secure the bottom in the same way. Hold the glued seamlines together with two hands. Place the arc, seam side down, on wax paper and remove the clips. Clean off any excess glue with a clean cloth, then place weights along the back seam (see figure 6) and let dry.

7. Apply glue around the arc's bottom inside edge, then put the bottom ring in and clip with bulldog clips (see figure 7). Make sure the edge of the paper is tight on the ring, working with one side of the frame against your body. Glue the top ring in place in the same way (see figure 8). You may need to work with the rings to get them in place properly. Allow glue to dry.

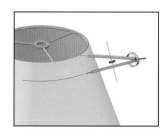

Figure 9

10. Working in 10-inch (25 cm) increments, apply glue to the lower half of the binding, and finger-press the binding in place. Repeat until you reach the back seam, then cut away the excess binding perpendicular to the shade's edge. Let dry.

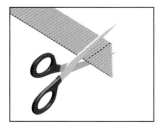

Figure 10

11. Cut v-shaped slashes in the binding to ease all points where the fitter wires connect to ring wires (see figure 11).

12. Apply a thin coat of glue to the inside of the remaining ribbon. Roll and mold the binding over the top of the wire. Crease the edge of the binding snugly and remove any excess glue. Repeat this process for the bottom edge, omitting the slashes.

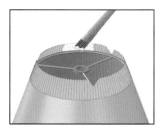

Figure 11

Pairing Shades and Bases

Choosing the perfect shade for a lamp base—or choosing the perfect base for a shade—can be challenging. The right match can guarantee that your lamp will be a star; the wrong match may doom it to a dark corner of the room. This chart offers suggestions for combining shades and bases with complementary proportions. Consider, too, the effect of pairing a brightly colored base with a brightly colored shade, or an understated base with a more bold shade, or a high-tech base with a delicate-looking shade. Choices, choices, choices!

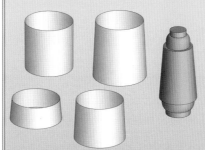

Bell-shaped shades look attractive on vase- and urn-style bases.

Cone-shaped shades tend to look best with bases that are wider and heavier at the bottom.

Drum shapes work well on column lamps and bases that are heavier at the bottom.

Empire shades look great with vases and Early American-style bases.

Hexagon shades flatter Early-American-style bases.

Oval shades complement bases that have oval lines.

Chimney shades work well with Colonial and Provincial bases.

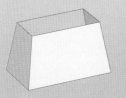

Square and rectangular shades work well with square and almost-square bases.

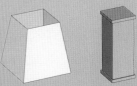

T he lamps included in this section have been inspired by ordinary objects. We have discovered that you can make a lamp from just about anything!

Clockwise: 1. High-heel lamp designed by Kyle Spencer. 2. Fishing basket lamp; courtesy of Laura Dover. 3. Garden sconce; courtesy of Diane Weaver. 4. Tin can lamp; collection of Ronnie Meyers. 5. Phone lamp; courtesy of Jane LaFerla. 6. Copper kettle lamp; collection of Ronnie Meyers. 7. Dutch shoe lamp; collection of Stuf Antiques 8. Duck Decoy lamp; courtey of Stuf Antiques

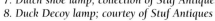

COMMON OBJECTS

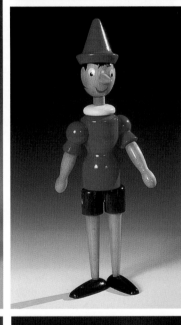

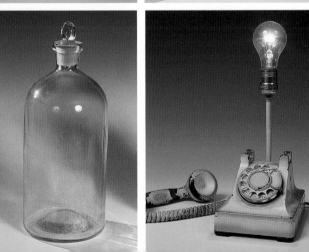

Vase Lamp with Paper Mache Shade

Designer ▪▪ *Diane Weaver*

The scene-stealer here is definitely the shade, bestowing on the inexpensive, new vase the mystique of a valued artifact.

What You Need

30-inch (75 cm) square of flexible cardboard (not corrugated)

clear, self-adhesive shelf paper

masking tape

large paper clips

large plastic bucket

4-6 sheets of translucent handmade paper, 30 x 40 inches (75 x 100 cm)

fabric stiffener

large, medium, and small lamp shade fitter rings; small ring should have
    connector for a harp

bottle lamp kit

harp

finial

light bulb

craft glue

craft knife

paintbrush with 3-inch -wide (8 cm) brush

pencil

compass

drill with masonry bit

What You Do

1. Draw a 30-inch-diameter (75 cm) circle on the cardboard and cut it out.

2. Cut a small wedge out of the circle from the outside to the center point. Carefully slice off one layer of the cardboard on one side of the missing wedge, so that the overlap of the cardboard won't be too thick at the seam.

3. Cover the entire cardboard pattern on both sides with the self-adhesive shelf paper, allowing the sticky paper to seal in a ¼-inch (6 mm) overhang. This will keep the cardboard form dry and reusable.

4. Shape the cardboard pattern into a cone of the desired diameter. Paper clip the edges together at the outside, and neatly tape the seam. Place the cone over a tall bucket so that the form's edges don't touch anything.

5. Tear the handmade paper into triangular strips. Apply a coat of fabric stiffener to the cone, then place a paper strip on a section of the cone, then coat the paper with another layer of stiffener. Proceed in this manner until you have covered the cone with one layer of paper and stiffener. Repeat this process until you have built up six layers of stiffened paper, making sure the total number of layers is equal all the way around the cone. Let the torn edges of the paper overhang ½-inch (1.5 cm) below the bottom of the form to give the finished shade an unmistakable handmade look. Reserve half a sheet of paper for later to cover the rings that will go inside the shade.

6. Allow the shade to dry for several days before attempting to remove it from the form. To do so, cut off the top of the shade first by using a compass to draw a circle of the desired diameter at the top; then use a craft knife to cut the small cone loose.

7. To ensure that your shade keeps its shape in humid weather, glue fitter rings on the inside of the shade, one near the bottom and one near the middle. Cover the rings with handmade paper, glued on with a layer of fabric stiffener. Glue a ring near the top of the shade that accommodates a harp and finial.

8. Drill a hole in the vase at or near the bottom. Drill slowly, using a minimum of pressure. Use water to keep the tip of the drill bit cool.

9. Wire the lamp following the instructions that come with the kit. Screw in the bulb, and attach the shade and finial.

High-Tech Billiards Lamp

Designer ▪▪ *Olivier Rollin*

Topped by a paper and wire shade, this dramatic lamp has a unique base
made from old disc drums and painted cue balls.

What You Need

cardboard

masking tape

trash bag

water-based glue

translucent paper

18-gauge wire

(2) disc drums, one slightly larger than the other

(3) cue balls

metallic luster wax

(3) pieces of metal pipe, 1 inch wide x 2 inches long (2.5 x 5 cm)

epoxy

3-inch (8 cm) metal crossbar with corresponding cut threaded wire and nut

lamp parts; see pages 9-10

spatula or ruler

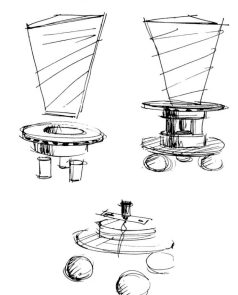

What You Do

Making the Shade

The shade for this lamp was designed
by making a triangular form to shape
the paper. The dimensions and shape
of your shade will depend on the base
you have found. Be sure to leave
enough room for a bulb to fit through
each end, and allow a safe distance
between the sides and the bulb for
ventilation.

1. Begin by taping cardboard into the
size and shape you desire for your finished shade.

2. Seal the exterior of the form by
covering it with the plastic from a
trash bag; use tape to hold the plastic
in place.

3. Coat the form with a water-based
glue, leaving the top and bottom of

the triangle uncovered, and loosely
wrap the form in paper.

4. Coil wire around this first layer,
stretching it from the top to the bottom. Brush on another coat of water-
based glue until the entire form is
covered. Layer again with paper, covering the wire, and coat this outer
layer with glue. Set aside to dry.

Assembling the Base

1. Treat the parts for the base as
desired by removing rust or coating
the parts with a metallic wax. Coat
the cue balls and metal pipe with
metallic luster wax to produce a
bronze finish.

2. Use epoxy to glue the three cue
balls at equal distances to the bottom
of the larger disc drum.

3. Epoxy the cut pipe in three places
between the top and bottom drums.
When choosing where to position the
pipe pieces, be aware that you can
hide the lamp cord by passing it
through one of the pipes and out a
hole in the bottom base.

4. Screw the threaded wire into the
hole in the crossbar, and use epoxy to
glue this unit across the center of the
top drum. Attach the socket and
bulb. Pass the lamp cord through the
threaded wire and into the base.

5. Pry the dry shade from the form
with a spatula or ruler. Remove the
plastic layer and discard it.

6. Position the finished shade in the
opening of the base; check for proper
bulb ventilation.

Tin Can Tower

Designer ▪▪ *David Williamson*

Quirky and playful, this tower of a lamp features tin cans that once held assorted Asian delicacies. Make your lamp with your favorite colorful cans, from Italian tomatoes to gourmet cat food!

What You Need

assorted aluminum cans in various sizes, empty and clean
masking tape
pencil
tin globe or other round accessory to cover finial
rubber ball or other round item for a pull-chain
wooden base
lamp parts and one-way pull chain; see pages 9-10
lamp shade
harp bottom and harp
finial
light bulb
large nail or center punch
reamer
hacksaw
file

What You Do

1. Try different ways to stack the cans until you find an arrangement you like. Mark each can with masking tape and number it to indicate its position in the stack.

2. Start from the bottom of the stack. Locate the center point on the top on each can. Using a nail or center punch, punch a hole through the top of each can.

3. Use the reamer to enlarge the hole to ⅜-inch (9 mm) wide.

4. As each can is punched and the hole enlarged, slide it down the threaded rod.

5. With all the cans in place, slide the rod through the lamp base and tighten with a nut and washer.

6. At the top of the stack, place another washer, then the harp bottom.

7. Mark the threaded rod ⅜-inch (9 mm) above the harp bottom. Cut off the remaining rod with the hacksaw. Lightly file the edge of the rod to ease screwing on of the socket.

8. Tighten the socket on the rod. This will snug the cans together.

9. Run the lamp cord up the rod from the bottom. Wire the lamp.

10. Install the harp, screw in the bulb, and attach the shade and finial.

11. Attach a small rubber ball to the pull chain by punching a hole through the top and threading the chain through.

Southwestern Flowerpots

Designer ▪▪ *Cathy Smith*

Terra-cotta pots make the ideal background for a sand painted, Native American design. The result is a stunning and easy-to-make table lamp.

What You Need

3 terra-cotta flowerpots, 3 inches (8 cm) high

1 terra-cotta saucer, 6 inches (15 cm) wide

waterproof adhesive that works on porous and non-porous materials

lamp parts; see pages 9-10

masking tape

white charcoal pencil

transfer paper and pencil (optional)

matte-finish acrylic decoupage medium

craft sand in colors of your choice

several applicator bottles

lamp shade

several feathers and beads (optional)

finial

light bulb

drill with ¼-inch (6 mm) bit

#4 and #1 round paintbrushes

toothpicks

eraser

craft sticks

craft knife

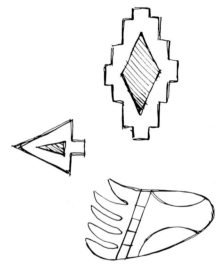

What You Do

Assembling the Base

1. Assemble the pots, as shown in figure 1.

2. Wire the lamp. Use glue to reinforce the nut that holds the lamp assembly together.

3. Drill a ¼ inch (6 mm) half-circle hole in the saucer rim so the cord can pass through. Tape the cord to the bottom so it doesn't twist up while you are decorating the base.

Decorating the Base

1. Draw the pattern onto the terra cotta surface with white charcoal pencil. Native American designs are available in pattern books. You can use a copier to shrink or expand the designs and then use transfer paper and a pencil to trace these designs on your surface.

2. Use the #4 round brush to apply decoupage medium to the pattern. You need to apply the sand before the medium dries. Work in a 2-inch (5 cm) square area at a time, using one color of sand at a time, on one vertical section of the lamp base at a time. Apply two to three coats of medium/sand in order to obtain good coverage. The second and third coats are much easier and faster to apply. Allow each coat to be reasonably dry and the finished section to be completely dry before moving on to the next section. The decorated surface is easily damaged before it's completely dry, but solid as a rock after. Blow off excess sand between coats and be sure to recycle the sand.

3. Repeat the above process area by area, section by section, and color by color.

4. After all the designs are completed and thoroughly dry, erase any stray pencil lines and brush away loose, excess sand.

5. Double coat both the sanded and the bare areas with matte decoupage medium.

Decorating the Shade

1. If you want, you can decorate the shade by gluing on a few feathers and beads.

2. Screw in the light bulb. Attach the shade and finial.

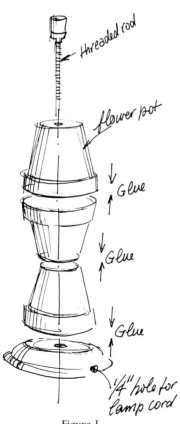

Figure 1

Hanging-Gear Lamp

Designer ▪▪ *Olivier Rollin*

It's easy to create a terrific hanging lamp by combining an old-fashioned glass insulator and an aluminum gear.

What You Need

glass electric insulator
found metal object with a hollow center into which the glass insulator will fit
silicone glue*
empty, clean aluminum can
lamp parts with ⅜ x 1½ inch- (9 mm x 4 cm) lamp nipple and
    (2) matching nuts, and clip-in lamp socket; see pages 9-10
light bulb
picture-frame hanging wire
drill and assorted bits
wire cutter
*available in hardware stores

What You Do

1. Drill three ⅛-inch (3 mm) holes at equal distances through the top of the metal object. Later, you will thread the wire through these holes in order to suspend the lamp.

2. Use silicone glue to attach the glass insulator to the metal object so that the open end fits inside the center and the rest of the insulator hangs below the base.

3. While the glue sets, drill a hole in the bottom of the aluminum can wide enough to accommodate the lamp cord.

4. Drill a hole in the top of the can for the nipple to fit through. Also, drill a few holes around the surface of the can for ventilation, perhaps in a decorative pattern.

5. Insert the nipple into the hole in the top of the can. Fasten it in place by screwing one nut on the inside of the can and one on the outside.

6. Screw the socket to the nipple.

7. Attach the lamp cord, and thread it through the hole in the bottom of the can.

8. Screw in the bulb.

9. The can rests on top of the base, slightly suspended inside the center opening of the metal object, directly above the glass insulator. The light bulb should not touch the glass. For additional support, you can fashion two beads from silicone glue, and place one on each side of the can to create friction between the can and the inside rim of the opening.

10. Measure three pieces of wire to the desired length for hanging the lamp, plus a few extra inches. Cut the wire to length, and thread each piece through one of the drilled holes. Slip the beads on the wire so that they will hold the found object in place; use silicone glue to adhere the beads to the wire. Gather the ends of the wire, keeping the lamp cord in the center, and knot the wire into a loop for hanging the finished lamp.

Stacked Gift Boxes

Designer ▪▪ *Sheila Ennis Schulz*

Made with stacked gift boxes, this cleverly designed lamp is both elegant and much sturdier than it looks.

What You Need

3 cardboard boxes with lids in graduated sizes*
gold acrylic spray paint
glazing medium with light brown tint
acrylic gold paint
spray polyurethane
wooden drawer handles
dark red spray paint (or color to match cord and tassels)
resealable plastic bags weighted with rocks or sand
lamp parts; see pages 9-10
white craft glue
10 yards (9.15 m) of cording
2 tassels to match cording
paper lamp shade in neutral color with clip-on fitter wire to accommodate finial
finial
light bulb
paintbrushes
sponge
drill and ⅜-inch (9 mm) bit
*available at art-supply stores

What You Do

1. Glaze the boxes and lids with the glazing medium.

2. Apply the gold paint with a sponge, highlighting the edges. Allow the boxes to dry completely.

3. Spray the boxes with polyurethane to protect the finish.

4. Spray the wooden feet with dark red paint.

5. Drill a ⅜-inch (9 mm) hole through the center of each box and lid.

6. Place the rod through the bottom box first, then weight the box with a plastic bag filled with rocks or sand.

7. Place the remaining two boxes and lids onto the rod. Cap off the rod and tighten it.

8. Assemble the lamp components and wire the lamp.

9. Glue the feet to the bottom of the stacked boxes.

10. Tie cording around the boxes in gift-wrapping fashion. Attach the tassels to the ends of the cords.

11. Screw in the bulb and attach the shade and finial.

Metal Mesh Lamp

Designer ▪▪ *Olivier Rollin*

The designer created this shimmering, elegant mood lamp by treating
humble metal screen as if it were fine silk.

What You Need

found metal base with a hollow center

mosquito screen or wire mesh

metallic wax (optional)

10-gauge wire

lamp socket and cord

halogen projector bulb

fluorescent or bronze spray paint

steel wool or wire brush

black ribbon, 1 inch (2.5 cm) wide

heavy-duty sewing needle and thread

craft glue

wire cutter

scissors

paintbrush

Metal Mesh Lamp

What You Do

Preparing the Base

1. Prepare the base as desired by removing tarnish or applying metallic wax.

1. Fashion a wire circle to fit securely inside the base. Set the lamp components inside this wire ring inside the base. Be sure that the projector bulb will fit through the wire ring, and leave room for adequate ventilation. Pass the lamp cord out the bottom of the base.

Making the Shade

1. Cut the wire mesh in the shape of a circle as large or small as desired. Highlight the edge by sewing or gluing on black ribbon. You could also trim the shade with decorative paper or weave wire around the edge.

2. Gather the mesh circle at its center to create a point, and clip 1 to 3 inches (2.5 to 8 cm) below this point. Paint this cut-off tip with fluorescent or metallic paint, and set it aside to dry.

3. The shade is made to rest inside the base, without being permanently attached to it. For stability, secure the wire mesh to the wire ring by binding with more wire. Push the ring and the attached mesh into the top of the base. Finish the lamp by placing the colored mesh tip on top of the hole in the center of the shade.

Bird Cage Lamp

Designer ▪▪ *Diane Weaver*

The designer transformed an old bird cage into a beautiful lamp that provides a gentle, glowing light.

What You Need

old wooden bird cage
decorative paper
white craft glue
lamp parts;see pages 9-10
low-watt bulb
scissors
drill and assorted bits

What You Do

1. Remove the bottom of the bird cage.

2. Cut the paper to fit one section of the cage at a time.

3. Apply glue to the edges of the paper and press the paper into position on the inside of the cage. Continue gluing on the paper until all the sides and the top of the cage are covered.

4. Drill a hole in the bottom center of the cage to fit the lamp components.

5. Wire the lamp and screw in the bulb.

6. Re-assemble the cage so that you can easily replace the bulb through the door or by removing the bottom of the cage.

Twin Topiaries

Designer ▪▪ *Karyn Sanders*

This pair of terra cotta lamps strikes a lovely topiary pose, and can be easily customized with your favorite flowers and ribbons.

What You Need

(1 or 2) 4-inch (10 cm) clay pots
green water-based paint
black marker
plastic electric Christmas candle
masking tape
plaster of Paris
old plastic container

small amount of sheet moss
craft glue
quick-set epoxy
silk flowers of your choice (about 15 blooms)
(1 or 2) 5-inch (13 cm) clip-on lamp shade
1 yard (.95 meters) of wired ribbon
1½ inch (4 cm) paintbrush

rat tail file
coping saw or mat knife
flathead screwdriver
hot-glue gun and glue sticks
old spoon

What You Do

Making the Base

1. Lightly dip the paintbrush into the green paint and wipe off any excess with a paper towel so that the brush is almost dry. Drag the brush around the circumference of the pot to give it a slightly aged look.

2. Turn the pot upside down. Using the file, make a groove in the bottom rim of the pot for the lamp cord to lay under.

3. Measure in 1½ inches (4 cm) on each side of the plastic candle base and mark the area. Use a coping saw or mat knife to trim off the excess. Insert the candle base into the terra cotta pot to check for fit. If the fit is not snug, remove the candle base and trim or file again.

4. Use the screwdriver to gently pry the light bulb holder out of the candle. With the screwdriver, open the clip that holds the cord. Be careful not to break the plastic. Remove the

cord, gently pulling it out of the candle.

5. Insert the candle base into the pot, making sure the base is level. Use hot glue where the plastic touches the inside of the pot to temporarily hold the candle base in place.

6. Thread the cord up through the hole in the bottom of the terra cotta pot and into the candle section. Replace the cord into the clip and snap shut. Replace the light bulb holder in the candle section, gently pulling the cord so that any excess is outside the candle section.

7. Plug in the lamp to make sure the cord is clipped in properly and works.

8. Unplug the cord, and tape a piece of duct tape or masking tape over the bottom of the hole.

9. Mix a small amount of plaster of Paris, according to package directions. It should have a mud-like consistency. Spoon it into the pot, ½ inch (1.5

cm) from the top. Allow the plaster to dry.

10. Using white glue, cover the candle section with a thin layer of sheet moss. Trim excess moss away from the bulb area. Hot-glue the moss to cover the plaster.

11. Wipe the groove on the bottom of the pot with a damp paper towel. Allow to dry. Using epoxy, glue the cord into the groove on the bottom of the pot.

Decorating the Shade

1. Remove the flower petals from their stems.

2. Use hot glue to attach the petals to the shade until the shade is completely covered. You can go back and fill in any spaces with the smaller flowers.

3. Tie a ribbon of your choice around the base.

Library Lamp

Designer ▪▪ *Jim Muesing*

Old novels give new meaning to a novelty lamp. This handsome reading light adds a rich glow to any room and encourages everyone to read a good book.

What You Need

several old hardback books*

clear water-based sealer

white craft glue

1¼ inch (3.5 cm) hardwood board**

wood stain

shellac or finish

wood, plastic, or metal tube, 2 inches (5 cm) wide

drawing or design for lamp stem

acrylic polymer medium (optional)

lamp parts; see pages 9-10

lamp shade with clip-on fitter wire that accommodates a finial

finial

fine-grade sandpaper

paintbrush

scissors

saw

drill with ¼-inch (6 mm) and 1-inch (2.5 cm) bits

router

*Look for old books at flea markets and yard sales. Envision how they will look stacked together, in terms of their size, age, and color.

**The length and width of the board should be 2 inches (5 cm) greater than the largest book. Bases can be purchased at lamp-supply stores.

What You Do

Making the Base

1. Stack the books in a pleasing arrangement, glue them together, and allow them to dry.

2. Coat the stacked books with water-based sealer. This protects the books with a dull finish that preserves the antique look.

3. Cut the hardwood board or buy it to size.

4. Drill a hole through the middle of the stack of books and the hardwood base, using a ¼-inch (6 mm) drill bit.

5. Drill another ¼ inch (6 mm) hole in the wood base to run the lamp cord from the center hole out through the side of the base.

6. Using a 1-inch (2.5 cm) bit, drill a hole ½-inch (1.5 cm) deep into the bottom of the base, centered over the ¼-inch (6 mm) hole. This creates the space for the screw, washer, and nut that bolt the lamp parts together.

7. Use a router to carve off the top edges of the wood base. Sand the base smooth.

8. Stain the wood with clear shellac.

Making the Stem

1. You have several options here, beginning with the type of material you choose for the stem. First, cut the wood, metal, or plastic tube to length. The exact measurement will depend on the height of the stack of books and the size and shape of the lamp shade.

2. If your stem is a hollowed wooden dowel, you might choose to simply stain the wood the color of the base. Another option is to paint the stem a color that complements the books or ties in with a color in the room where the lamp with sit.

3. If you want a decorative image on the stem, be prepared to devote another day to the project. First choose your image, design, or pattern to match the style of the lamp.

4. Using an acrylic polymer medium, heavily coat the paper image. Allow it to dry thoroughly. Re-coat the paper, allow it to dry, and re-coat it a third time.

5. When the coating is clear and dry to the touch, soak the coated paper in water. Leave it submerged until you can scrape or peel off the paper. You should now be able to see that the image has transferred to the clear polymer medium.

6. Cut the rubbery image to fit the length and circumference of the lamp stem. Since the image is transparent, the color of the stem will create the negative space. You might want to paint the tube ahead of time.

7. Glue the image to the stem by painting a fresh coat of polymer onto the stem and then wrapping the image around it.

Assembling the Lamp

1. Align the ¼-inch (6 mm) holes in the books and the wood base. Once positioned, turn the books askew to add interest.

2. Assemble the lamp components. Screw in the bulb, and attach the lamp shade and finial.

Raku Pot in Paper Mache Base

Designer ▪▪ Diane Weaver

Throw a warm spotlight on a favorite ceramic pot, vase, or sculpture by nesting it in a paper mache base, and topping it with a gorgeous handmade shade.

What You Need

ceramic pot, vase, or sculpture
spool of 12-gauge wire
plaster-impregnated fabric wrap
paper mache pulp
acrylic paints in black, turquoise, and gold
satin polyurethane
block of wood to fit inside pot
½-inch (1.5 cm) copper pipe, 12 inches (30 cm) long
lamp parts; see pages 9-10
wire lamp shade form that accommodates a finial

handmade paper
plain paper to make a pattern for the shade
craft glue
large paper clips
fabric stiffener
light bulb
finial
paintbrushes
scissors
drill with ½-inch (1.5 cm) mortar bit

What You Do

Making the Base

1. Using 12-gauge wire, form an armature to fit your ceramic pot, similar to the one shown in the drawing. Allow space for the pot to fit snugly in the base after the armature has been covered with paper mache.

2. Wrap the armature with plaster-impregnated fabric wrap, and let it dry.

3. Apply paper mache pulp to the armature, smoothing and forming it as desired. Let it dry thoroughly.

4. Paint the armature with black acrylic paint and let dry. Then paint over it with a thin coat of turquoise paint. Let dry. Finally, dry-brush the base with gold paint.

5. Slowly drill a hole through the bottom of the raku pot, using water to keep the drill bit cool. While you

drill, support the pot base from the inside with a block of wood.

6. Assemble the lamp, slipping the threaded rod inside the copper pipe.

Making the Shade

1. To avoid a costly mistake, first make a pattern for the shade out of plain paper, making sure it's large enough to allow the paper to wrap around the wire frame at the bottom and top of the shade.

2. After cutting the paper shape from the handmade paper, glue it as tightly as possible to the wire frame. Use paper clips to hold the edges of the paper over the edges of the frame while the glue dries. See pages 19 to 21 for more details.

3. To finish and protect the shade and to make the paper drum tight, brush

on a layer of fabric stiffener on both sides of the paper.

4. Screw in the light bulb and attach the finial.

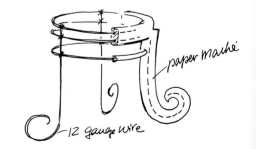

paper mache

12 gauge wire

Mighty Metal Base with Paper Shade

Designer ▪▪ *Olivier Rollin*

The designer created this handsome floor lamp by making a paper and lath shade to tower over the found metal base.

What You Need

large, heavy metal base
2 metal electrical conduits, 2 inches (5 cm) in diameter
4 metal brackets with matching screws and nuts
300-watt halogen bulb and fixture
1 sheet of diamond lath
spray adhesive
paintbrush
water-based glue
translucent paper
2 heavy-duty metal clamps
steel wool or steel brush
drill and bit that matches screw size
straightedge
wire cutters

What You Do

Making the Base

1. Brush the surface of the base with steel wool or a steel brush to remove any tarnish.

2. As shown in the photo above right, the electrical conduits are attached to the base with four metal brackets. Use two brackets for each conduit and space them a few inches apart. Mark and drill the holes for the bracket screws. Place the brackets over the conduits and screw them to the base.

3. Attach the halogen bulb fixture to each conduit at the open end of the frame so that the bulb shines downward, as shown in the photo below.

Making the Shade

1. To make the shade framework, fold and bend the lath by hand. A straight-edge is helpful for creating smooth creases and folds.

2. When you're satisfied with the shape of the frame, spray it with adhesive, and loosely wrap the paper around the lath. The paper doesn't have to be cut exactly to form; in fact, a few overlaps add to the texture of the finished shade.

3. Brush the paper with water-based glue until it's saturated. While the paper is wet, you may decorate the shade by pressing on additional pieces of confetti paper, leaves, or other thin, light appliqués. The glue will cause the paper to shrink against the frame and enhance its translucency.

4. As shown in the photograph below, attach a clamp between each conduit and the inside edge of the shade. This method allows you to easily remove the shade.

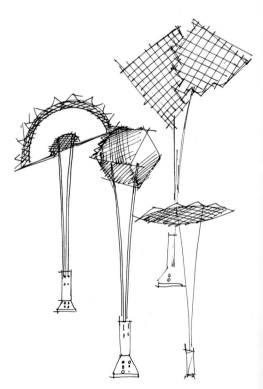

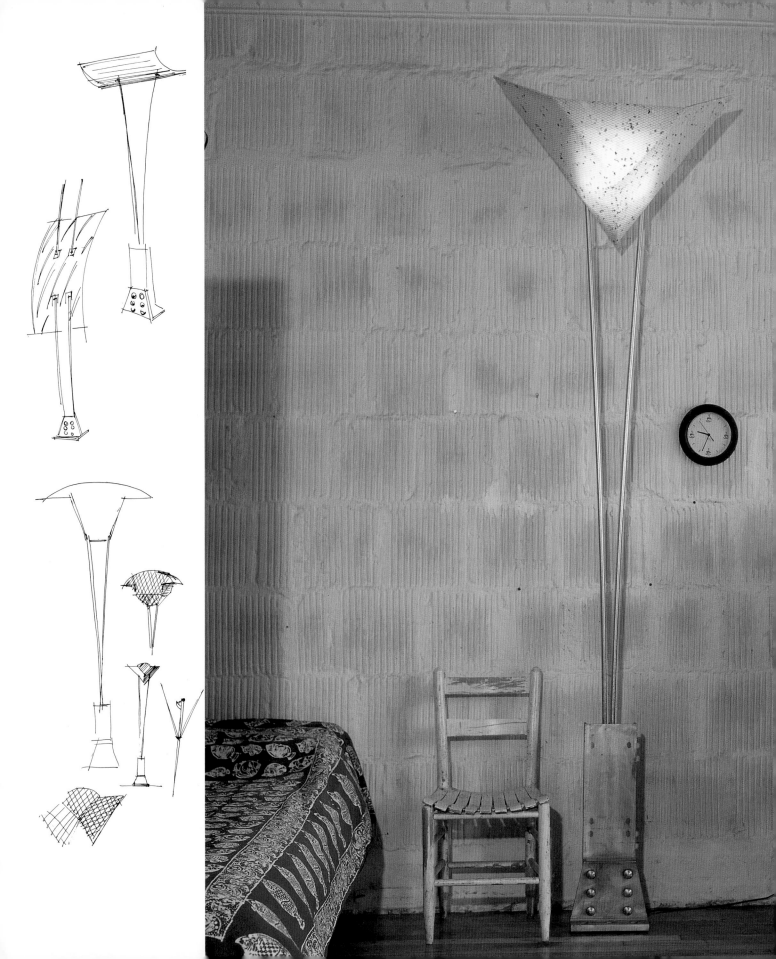

Coffeepot Wizard

Designer ▪▪ *Bobby Hansson*

Perfect as a night light, this delightful tin wizard will warm up a room and bring a smile to your face. (You may have to turn the book upside down to appreciate this one!)

What You Need

aluminum coffeepot

assorted disk-shaped metal objects for
    the eyes

screws

scrap of wood

sheet of tin

lamp parts; see pages 9-10

light bulb

acrylic paints

hammer

drill with assorted bits

screwdriver

metal cutters

awl

sandpaper

paintbrushes

What You Do

1. Use the hammer to dent the coffeepot lid so that one side caves in slightly. Fit this edge at a slight angle inside the top of the coffeepot.

2. Drill holes where you want the eyes to be positioned. Attach the metal disks with screws.

3. Drill a ½-inch (1.5 cm) hole through the bottom of the coffeepot.

4. Drill a ½-inch (1.5 cm) hole through the center of the scrap of wood. Sand the wood and paint it. Let it dry.

5. Wire the lamp by running the rod through the hole in the bottom of the pot, the hole in the lid, and the wooden base. Attach the socket to the bottom of the pot with screws.

6. Paint the coffeepot and lid and let it dry.

7. Shape the sheet of tin into a cone and rivet the edges together. Use the awl and the drill to make holes in the wizard's hat. The holes in this tin hat form a star lamp, featuring the Big Dipper in the front.

8. Use scraps of tin to make a hoop and two side panels. Use screws to attach the panels to the hoop and then to the sides of the tin cone (see photo below).

9. Paint the tin hat and let it dry.

10. Screw in the light bulb. Position the tin hat so the metal hoop rests just inside the rim of the coffeepot.

Colander Trio

Designer ▪▪ *Pamella Wilson*

Made from three colanders, this whimsical lamp emits diffuse light through the holes, creating a starry night effect.

What You Need

(3) stainless steel colanders, (2) large and (1) small
(2) #6 wing nuts
(2) #6 flathead screws, ½ inch (1.5 cm) long
several strands of medium-weight wire
lamp parts with candelabra base and snap-in socket; see pages 9-10
drill with ¼-inch (6 mm) and ½-inch (1.5 cm) bits
ball peen hammer
pliers
screwdriver

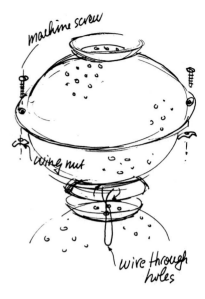

Figure 1

What You Do

1. On one side of each large colander, drill ¼-inch (9 mm) holes approximately 1 inch (2.5 cm) from the handles for insertion of the screws, as shown in figure 1. When completed, this will become the back part of the lamp.

2. In the center bottom portion of one of the large colanders (this will be the middle colander), drill a ½-inch (1.5 cm) hole, as shown in figure 1. Use the ball peen hammer to enlarge the hole to a 1-inch (2.5 cm) diameter.

3. In the colander base you just drilled, use the pliers to bend an opening for the lamp cord, as shown in figure 2. Repeat this procedure with the small colander. Make sure the openings match when the colanders are put base to base. (The smaller colander will be turned upside down and matched to the base of the middle colander.)

4. Wire the small colander to the middle colander by threading wire shaped

Figure 2

into U-pins through many of the holes in the colander bottoms. Twist tie each connection tightly so the colanders won't slip off one another. Clip the wire ends with pliers.

5. Insert the snap-in socket through the 1-inch (2.5 cm) hole in the middle colander, as shown in figure 3. Gently squeeze the metal ears on the socket. Use the bent opening on the colanders to suspend the cord.

6. For the top part of the lamp, turn the other large colander upside down and use the screws and wing nuts to attach it to the middle colander.

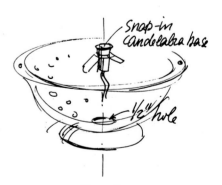

Figure 3

Coiled Lamp

To create this handsome lamp, the designer paired a recycled metal coil with a paper and wire shade. When light passes through the shade, the entire lamp casts a warm glow.

Designer ▪ ▪ Olivier Rollin

What You Need

coiled metal object
heavy cardboard
plastic trash bag
masking tape
wood glue
3 feet (.9 m) heavy-gauge wire
translucent paper
metal lath
lamp socket and cord
low-watt bulb
craft knife
paintbrush
spatula or ruler
wire cutter

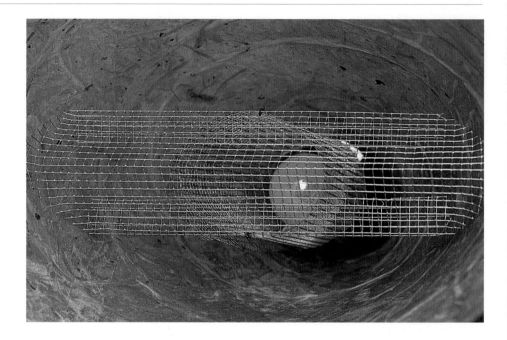

What You Do

Making the Shade

1. Make a cone-shaped form out of the cardboard that will work with the size of the coiled metal object you are using as the base. Be sure to leave enough room for a bulb to fit through each end of the shade, and allow a safe distance between the sides and the bulb for ventilation. Tape a trash bag to the outside of the form.

2. Brush the form with wood glue, and loosely wrap the sticky surface with translucent paper. Overlapping the paper will create attractive patterns in the finished shade.

3. Wrap the wire in a coil-like fashion around the paper, stretching it from one end of the form to the other.

4. Brush this first layer of paper and wire with a generous coating of glue; then wrap a second layer of paper around the form. The wire will now be sandwiched between the two layers.

5. Coat the form with glue again and allow to dry.

6. When the shade is dry, carefully remove it from the form by using a spatula or ruler. Remove the plastic wrapping and discard it.

Wiring the Lamp

1. As shown in the photo above, the bulb and socket are suspended within a cage inside the finished shade. Use the metal lath to create a triangular cage; then wedge it inside the shade. Fashion a square cage in which to enclose the bulb and socket, and sus-pend it from the triangular cage. Be sure to leave room for ventilation between the bulb and shade as you design your housing for the electrical components.

2. Position the wired shade in the metal base. Allow the lamp cord to dangle through the bottom of the shade, down through the base.

AND ORDINARY

We feel a certain fondness for the lamps pictured here—probably because the ones we didn't buy at thrift stores and yard sales came from our very own homes where they served as loyal reading lamps, reliable accent lights and friendly chandeliers. We turned these plain, old, and, yes, ugly lamps over to several designers who gave them complete makeovers. You will be amazed at the results. So take a look around your house, search the attic and rummage sales, and give an ordinary lamp a chance to be truly extraordinary.

All That Jazz

Designer ▪▪ *Shelley Lowell*

Inspired by the decorative patterns on her Guatemalan bracelets, the designer transformed a very conservative lamp into a exuberant medley of color and texture.

What You Need

lamp in working condition
colorful, patterned bangle bracelets
black paper shade
stencil guide (optional)
pencil
tracing paper
white transfer paper
masking tape
acrylic paint to match bracelets
flat black paint for painting on metal
gesso
water-based polyurethane
6 black marbles
quick-drying epoxy for gluing glass
2 wooden balls, (1) 3/4 inch (2 cm) in
    diameter, (1) 2 inches (5 cm) in
    diameter
wood filler
paintbrushes
sandpaper
drill with 1/4-inch (6 mm) and 1/2-inch
    (1.5 cm) bits*

*Note: Check the diameter of the finial and the on/off switch knob, and match the size of the drill bit to them. This lamp had a 3-way switch, so there was an actual on/off knob. Lamps with only an on/off switch dont have knob handles; they have a switch you push in, so you won't be able to put a wooden ball on it.

What You Do

Painting the Shade

1. If you feel intimidated painting the polka dots freehand, use a stencil guide or bottle cap to draw the circles on tracing paper. Then, gently tape the tracing paper onto the shade and, using transfer paper, trace the circles onto the shade. Remove the tracing paper and paint the polka dots. Let the paint dry.

Decorating the Base

2. If your base has any metal parts, lightly sand them to remove the gloss.

3. Paint the wood parts with gesso. You may have to thin the gesso, according to the manufacturer's directions.

4. Paint the metal parts black with the metal paint.

5. Starting with the base, paint patterns inspired by your bracelets. You may want to draw out your design first. (Note: You don't need to prime the metal parts with gesso; once you paint them with metal paint, you can cover those areas with acrylic paint.)

6. Continue painting the entire lamp with patterns, and let dry overnight.

7. Coat the painted areas with polyurethane. Let dry 24 hours.

8. To glue on the marbles, first place the lamp on its side. You may have to prop the top part of the base on something so the main body of the lamp can be completely horizontal; this way the marbles won't roll around. You will be gluing one marble at a time. Mix a very small amount of epoxy. Dab a small amount where you want the marble. Immediately tape the marble in place until the glue sets. After each marble is set, turn the lamp and repeat this procedure until all the marbles are glued in various positions.

9. The finial on this lamp looked like a flat button. If this is the case with your lamp, find a bottle cap around the house into which the 2-inch (5 cm) wooden ball will fit securely. With masking tape, tape the ball into the cap so it won't roll around on a flat surface. Tape the cap with the ball in it onto a work surface. With the electric drill, using a drill bit that matches the diameter of the finial or a little larger, drill a hole so that the finial will fit in the hole. Put some wood filler in the hole, press the finial into it, wipe off the excess, and let harden. Do the same thing with the smaller wooden ball and the switch knob. (Note: On three-way switches, you can unscrew the knob, so you can glue the wood knob onto the knob of the lamp; this is an easier process.)

10. Sand the wood-filled area on each knob. Prime with gesso. Let dry. Then pick two colors from the lamp design and paint each knob a different color. When thoroughly dry (24 hours), coat knobs with polyurethane. Let dry. Put the knob on the switch.

11. Place the bracelets over the lamp and let them slide down and rest on the base, or let some hang on the marbles. This is a lamp you can play with, rearranging the bracelets just for fun. (Note: These woven bracelets are pliable, so they are easy to bend if necessary when putting them on the lamp.)

Biedermeier-Style Table Lamp

Designer ▪▪ *Sheila Ennis Schulz*

Similar to a showy style of furniture popular in Germany in the early 19th century, this refurbished lamp has a distinctly Biedermeier look, made even more impressive with an expensive Tiffany shade.

What You Need

old lamp in working condition
masking tape
black spray paint
furniture cream
new pull chain and harp
light bulb
Tiffany-style shade with mica trim
finial
sandpaper, 150 and 220 grit

What You Do

1. Sand off the old paint (this may take more effort than you think if you have a very rough surface.)

2. Tape off the wooden parts of the lamp, and spray the black parts with black paint. Let dry.

3. Polish the wooden parts with furniture cream.

4. Attach the new harp and pull chain.

5. Screw in the light bulb, and attach the shade and finial.

Note: this is the same lamp as shown on page 55!

Dutch Master Still Life

Designer ▪▪ *Dana Irwin*

With brush in hand and tongue in cheek, the designer transformed an old lamp with life-size fruit into a painted "masterpiece" that pays homage to the subject and colors used by Dutch artists, such as Rembrandt.

What You Need

old ceramic lamp in working condition
ceramic paint in colors of your choice*
ceramic conditioner
black acrylic paint
clear acrylic sealer
lamp shade
finial
light bulb
paintbrushes
*available in craft-supply stores

What You Do

1. Clean the lamp surface well and let it dry.

2. Ceramic paints are designed to be used with a special conditioner and sealer. Read the manufacturer's directions. Then apply the conditioner to the surface of the lamp.

3. Paint the lamp and let it dry.

4. Dry-brush the black paint over the surface to create highlights and shadows. Let dry.

5. Apply a coat of sealer and let dry.

6. Screw in the light bulb and attach the shade and finial.

Blue Willow Mosaic

Designer ▪▪ *Terry Taylor*

To transform a plain lamp into a personal expression, the designer used pieces of blue willow china to create a lovely mosaic.

What You Need

lamp in working condition
several china plates
cement mortar
rubber gloves
plastic containers
powdered grout
foam packaging material
sponges

lint-free rags
lamp shade
light bulb
finial
tile nippers
small plastic artist's palette knife
craft knife

What You Do

1. Using the tile nippers, begin cutting irregular pieces from the outer rim of one plate. Work inward toward the center flat portion of the plate; then cut the larger pieces into 1-inch (2.5 cm) pieces. Repeat this process with other plates until you have a good quantity of workable pieces.

2. Repeat step one with another plate, but this time be sure that you can put the pieces back together like a puzzle; these are the pieces that will re-create the plate in mosaic form on your lamp base.

3. Mix a small amount of cement mortar according to the manufacturer's directions. Starting with a small amount of water, add dry mortar until you have the consistency of thick mud. Allow the mixture to cure as recommended.

4. Using a palette knife, apply a ⅛-inch to ¼- inch (3 mm to 6 mm) coating of mortar to a small section in the center of the lamp base. Put a light coat of mortar on the back of each piece of china that you want in the center of the mosaic, and press it in place on the lamp base. Be sure to allow enough space between the pieces for the grout. Use the edge of your knife to remove excess mortar

from the crevices. Continue applying mortar and china pieces to small areas at a time until you have completed your design.

5. Allow the mosaic to dry for at least 24 hours.

6. Mix the powdered grout according to the manufacturer's instructions.

7. Cut the foam packaging material into 3- or 4-inch (8-10 cm) squares.

8. Use the foam squares to work the grout into the spaces between the china pieces. After allowing the grout to set up for about 15 minutes, remove any excess material with a barely damp sponge or lint-free rags. Allow the grout to cure for a couple of days.

9. Screw in the light bulb and attach the shade and finial.

The designer created a swirl mosaic pattern on this lamp.

Tinkerbell's Chandelier

Designer ▪▪ Shelley Lowell

This once-drab chandelier was given a generous sprinkling of fairy dust by a designer with a love of gauze, dazzling colors, and flashy beads.

What You Need

chandelier in working condition
10-gauge wire
ceiling hook
paint designed for use on metal; this color
*   should match the acrylic paint used*
as the base color
plaster impregnated fabric wrap
bowl of water
small sponges
gesso acrylic paint; pick two or three
*   colors that work well together*
beads, stones, and sequins
cyanoacrylate glue
various jewelry parts to make dangles
lightweight craft wire
earring wire (enough for each arm
*   of fixture)*
paintbrushes
heavy-duty sewing needle
round-nose jewelry pliers
tweezers

* available in craft-supply stores

What You Do

1. Mount a hook in the ceiling, preferably in a beam, and wrap 10-gauge wire around it. Hang the chandelier from the wire so that it hangs below table level; this setup makes it easy to work on the lamp.

2. Place drop cloths on the floor under the chandelier. Using the paint for metal, paint the chain and the plate that attaches to the ceiling. Let dry.

3. Take one strip of plaster wrap, about 12 inches (31 cm) long, and dip it in water. Squeeze out the excess water. Starting at the top of the fixture where the chain connects to the ring, wrap the center column with plaster fabric. Using as many 12-inch (31 cm) strips as needed, continue to wrap the center column. You may scrunch or pinch the gauze as you go to create an attractive pattern.

4. Wrap each arm of the chandelier with plaster fabric, starting where the arm joins the column. After the chandelier is completely wrapped, cut another strip for each arm. Loosely wrap the bottom, curved area of each arm so the plaster wrap looks draped, being careful to blend the strips so you can't see where one starts and another begins. Cut two more strips, long enough to go around the area on the center column where the arms connect. With the first strip, weave the plaster fabric over and under the arms around the column. Then, using the other strip, wrap in the opposite direction: under and over the arms around the column. Let the plaster wrap dry overnight.

5. Using a clean sponge, sponge the gesso on the fabric wrap. You may need to turn the chandelier upside down or crawl underneath to check all the angles to be sure it's completely covered with gesso. Let dry.

6. Thin the acrylic paint that will be the base color until it's the consistency of light cream. Pour some in a flat dish. Dip a clean sponge in the diluted paint, and sponge it onto the fixture. Again, you may need to turn the chandelier upside down or crawl

underneath, checking all angles to make sure it's completely covered with paint.

7. Sponge on the other color, lightly dabbing some areas and heavily dabbing other areas to create a blended effect. Work with the contours of your particular fixture. If you desire, blend on a third color.

8. Make "a dangle" to hang on the bottom of the curve of each arm using various jewelry parts. This is just like making the bottom part of an earring. (You may want to consult actual earrings for inspiration.) Use the sewing needle to make a hole in the gauze where you want the dangle to hang. Cut a 2-inch (5 cm) piece of craft wire. Insert it in the hole and into the wire of the dangle, and secure. Trim the wire, if necessary.

9. On your work surface, prop the chandelier on its side with a pillow. You may need additional props to keep the fixture horizontal and steady.

10. Use the tweezers to grip each bead, stone, and sequin. Glue them to the chandelier, turning the fixture as you work. With this lamp, the more the better!

Gilded Beauty

Designer: Terry Taylor

The designer transformed a humble lamp into one worthy of the respect of King Midas. Covered with a generous amount of "junk" jewelry and sprayed gold, the lamp is sure to light up any room.

What You Need

lamp in working condition

heaps of "junk" jewelry—pins, earrings, necklaces,
*   bracelets*

acrylic modeling paste

masking tape

gesso or acrylic base-coat paint

acrylic metallic gold paint

jewelry or wire cutters

flat-nosed jewelry pliers

small palette knife or similar tool

small paintbrushes

What You Do

1. Remove all pin backs, posts, and findings from the jewelry with wire or jewelry cutters and jewelry pliers. Think about what pieces will work well with each other.

2. Spread a generous amount of acrylic modeling paste about 1/16 inch (.25 cm) thick on a small area of the lamp base.

3. Spread a generous amount of modeling paste on the back of a piece of jewelry—flat earrings need less, for example, than a large domed brooch. Set it in place on top of the modeling-paste base; you don't need to push it in. Use the palette knife to remove excess modeling paste around the edges. When you've covered your work area with jewelry, let it dry for 24 hours. Thicker amounts of modeling paste require a longer drying period. Repeat steps 2 and 3 until the base is covered.

4. Coat the jewelry surface with acrylic gesso or base-coat paint. Dab the brush into the nooks and crannies to completely cover the jewelry. Allow the paint to dry.

5. Finish with at least two coats of metallic paint.

Fancy Hat Desk Lamp

Designer ▪▪ *Pat Scheible*

This campy little desk lamp—once all business—is now all dressed up with everywhere to go. The iridescent coloring and ruffled hat will brighten any work or living space.

What You Need

metal desk lamp in working condition*
all-purpose latex primer
black enamel spray paint
gold enamel spray paint
iridescent purple acrylic paint
gold wired ribbon (enough to fit twice the circumference of the shade)
craft glue
blue iridescent wired ribbon (same amount as gold ribbon)
"liquid crystal" cabochon (available in novelty stores)
black and gold braid
paintbrushes
hot-glue gun and glue sticks

*Look in thrift stores and at yard sales for lamps with clean lines.

What You Do

1. Coat the lamp with latex primer.

2. Spray the inside of the shade gold. Spray paint everything else black.

3. Daub the iridescent purple paint on top of the black paint. Let it dry.

4. Gather the gold wired ribbon into ruffles to fit the inside rim of the shade, and hot-glue it in place. Hot-glue a second row of ruffled ribbon, using the iridescent blue on the outside rim of the shade.

5. Hot-glue the liquid crystal cabochon to the top of the shade.

6. Hot-glue the black and gold braid around the ruffle and cabochon.
Note: The liquid crystal is heat sensitive, which means it will provide a handy light indicator: If the crystal is blue, it means the lamp is off; if the crystal is red, it means the lamp is on.

Gold Boudoir Lamp

Designer ▪▪ *Ellen Zahorec*

This glamorous vamp of a lamp lived for many years as a drab recluse. It's amazing what a little velvet and gold can do!

What You Need

lamp in working condition
fabric lamp shade
gold composition leaf
acrylic polymer
gold acrylic spray paint
velvet wire ribbon
2 soft paintbrushes
hot-glue gun and glue sticks

What You Do

1. Brush a coat of acrylic polymer on the base.

2. With your fingers, gently place a section of gold leaf on the damp sur-

face. Use the other paintbrush to brush on more gold leaf. Continue this procedure until the entire base is covered with gold leaf. Let dry.

3. Spray the lamp shade with gold paint and let dry.

4. Hot glue the crimped velvet ribbon to the shade and around the base. Note: The wire in the ribbon will get hot from the glue: be careful to not burn your fingers.

Chinese Decoupage

Designer ▪▪ *Sheila Ennis Schulz*

A Chinese motif and a handsome lamp shade turn a remarkably plain lamp into a remarkably beautiful accent light.

What You Need

rectangular wooden lamp in working condition
white craft glue
sheets of Chinese newspaper
walnut stain or water-based glazing medium
dark brown tint (available at paint stores)
black acrylic spray paint
square piece of wood, sized for the base to sit on
wood glue
harp and harp bottom
lamp shade finial, Oriental in style
light bulb
paintbrushes
craft knife

What You Do

1. Dilute the craft glue with water. Layer a sheet of Chinese newspaper onto the base in decoupage style. Add more layers in whatever design you like best. Trim any rough edges with the craft knife. Allow the glue to dry overnight.

2. Stain or glaze the entire surface of the base.

3. Attach the new harp and harp bottom.

4. Spray the square piece of wood black. Let dry.

5. Use wood glue to attach the black base to the bottom of the lamp base. Let dry.

6. Screw in the bulb. Attach the shade and finial.

Brass Lamp with Beaded Shade

Designer ▪▪ *Nancy McGaha*

The warm hues of the colored beads complement the brass base. Beading the shade with peyote stitch requires patience, but the result is a beautiful, one-of-a-kind lamp.

W h a t   Y o u   N e e d

small brass lamp base in working
condition
lamp shade wire frame that fits size of
lamp base
5-6 large containers of #6 Japanese
matte beads in various colors
beading thread
scissors

W h a t   Y o u   D o

Note: There are many excellent books that describe peyote stitch in detail. One such book is *Creative Bead Weaving* by Carol Wilcox Wells (Lark, 1996).

1. Starting from the top of the lamp shade wire frame, add beads until you reach the width you need, making sure your total is an even number.

2. To start the next row, pick up another bead and take the needle through the second bead from the end. In the example shown in figure 1, pick up bead #9 and go through bead #7.

3. As shown in figure 2, pick up bead #10 and stitch through bead #5. Continue until you reach the end of this row. Use a free-form design, adding color combinations randomly.

4. To turn and go back in the opposite direction, pick up bead #13 and stitch through the last bead in the

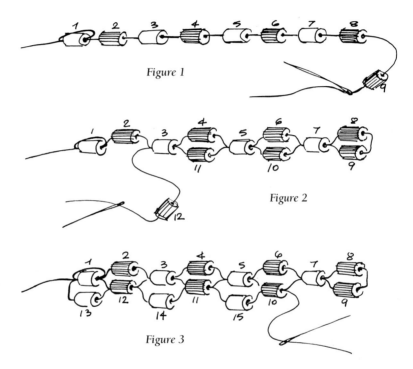

Figure 1

Figure 2

Figure 3

previous row, #12 (see figure 3).

5. Secure the last row of stitching to the bottom of the wire frame with thread.

6. If the stem of the lamp shows too much of the lamp workings around the light socket, you can adds rows of peyote stitching to this area, too. String beads onto the beading thread, and begin at the section where the lamp workings are exposed. The rows will pull tight as you work them around the lamp. Use only one color of beads to offset the variegated colors in the shade.

Country Makeover

Designer •• Cathy Smith

With romantic colors and fabrics, the designer turned an old brass floor lamp into a fetching and feminine country classic.

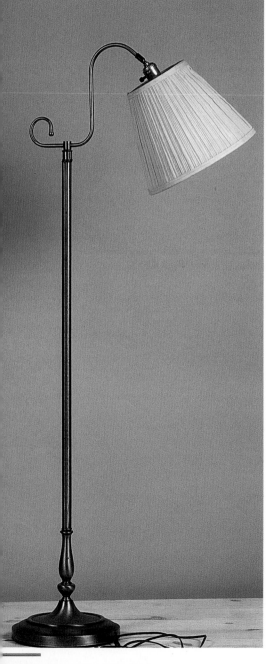

What You Do

1. Clean the lamp well to remove oil and dirt. Sand the surfaces lightly; then wipe clean to remove sanding debris.

2. Base coat the pole and base with enamel oil-base paint. Allow it to dry overnight. After drying, use steel wool to provide a receptive surface for a second coat; then wipe clean to remove sanding debris. Apply a second coat and allow it to dry overnight.

3. Cut the fabric lengthwise into sufficient 1-inch (2.5 cm) wide strips to spiral down the pole and to trim the bottom of the lamp shade. Put aside the strip for the shade.

4. Apply craft glue to the back of a fabric strip (you may want to do this in sections as the glue dries pretty quickly). Be sure to cover the entire back surface of the strip, with special attention to the edges. Spiral the fabric strip down the pole to the base. Smooth the fabric down firmly, but without stretching the fabric. (Excess glue can be removed after the decoupage compound and trim have been put on.) Trim any excess fabric.

5. Apply one coat of matte-finish decoupage compound to the fabric strip, being sure to cover the entire fabric surface, especially the edges. Again, don't worry about excess acrylic until later. Let the fabric dry completely.

6. Glue a ¼-inch (6 cm) braid to both sides of the fabric strip and let dry. Then use a damp cloth and gently but firmly rub off the excess glue and acrylic from the painted ares.

7. Cut a "doughnut" from the fabric to trim around the base (you may find it easier to do this in two pieces). Glue on the fabric as in step 3. Glue on the braid trim and let dry. Clean the painted areas with a damp cloth.

8. Paint the flowers on the pole and the base with white model paint. The flowers consist of five dots around a central dot.

Making the Lamp Shade

1. Gently take the old lamp shade apart and put the liner and cover materials aside. Clean any old material from the wire frames.

2. Place the old shade liner on top of the heavy white paper and trace the outline in pencil. Add ½ inch (2.5 cm) seam allowance. Cut out the shade. Repeat this process with the Japanese paper.

3. Thin the base coat to the consistency of a wash so that the shade will be translucent. Paint one side of the heavy white paper with wash and let it dry completely.

4. Using an old toothbrush and the accent colors, spatter paint on the Japanese paper.

5. Glue the sides of the heavy paper together, painted side facing out. Allow the seam to dry. Glue the liner to the frame as described on pages 19 to 21.

6. Use the decoupage compound to adhere the Japanese paper (spattered side out) to the shade liner. Work in 4-inch (10 cm) sections, brushing the decoupage compound onto the shade liner. Smooth on the cover paper and move to the next section. Continue until the shade is completely covered and let dry.

7. Thoroughly cover all surfaces of the cover paper with two coats of decoupage compound. Allow it to dry between coats.

8. Glue a 1-inch (2.5 cm) strip of fabric around the bottom of the shade.

9. Trim the top and bottom rim of the shade with the ½-inch (2.5 cm) braid, and the top of the fabric strip with the ¼-inch (6 mm) braid.

10. Glue the bird to the top of the lamp shade rim.

Shooting Star Lamp

Designer ▪▪ *Ellen Zahorec*

The designer made the stars come out on this thrift-store find, creating a delightful night light that any child would adore.

What You Need

lamp with wooden base in working condition
new or used white fabric lamp shade
glow-in-the-dark plastic stars
clear, adhesive shelf paper
pencil
black spray paint
gold dimensional fabric paint
enamel paint markers in gold and black
craft knife
scissors

What You Do

Painting the Shade

1. Place one of the plastic stars on the shelf paper and trace around it. Reposition it and trace the star again and again until you create a pattern you like.

2. Use the craft knife to cut out the stars: you now have a stencil.

3. Peel off the paper backing and adhere the stencil to the lamp shade, trimming the stencil to size.

4. Spray a light coat of black paint on the shade. Peel off the stencil.

Painting the Base

1. Spray the base black and let it dry.

2. Squeeze a dime-size amount of gold dimensional paint onto the base and press a plastic star on top of it. The gold paint will squish out around the stars and act as glue to hold the star to the base. Add more gold paint and more stars.

3. Use the enamel markers to add detail to the base and around the stars on the shade. Note: It is very important to use these markers in a well-ventilated room or outside.

4. Screw in the bulb and attach the shade.

Mardi Gras

Designer ▪▪ *Ellen Zahorec*

Jazz up an old lamp with souvenir beads from New Orleans or your treasured collection of costume jewelry. A little glue, a little paint, and get ready for the fireworks!

What You Need

lamp in working condition
white acrylic enamel spray paint
black acrylic enamel paint
black enamel paint pen
assorted strands of beads
black fabric lamp shade
dimensional fabric paints in bright colors
    that complement the beads
light bulb
scissors
paintbrushes
hot-glue gun and glue sticks

What You Do

Painting the Base

1. Spray the lamp stem white and let it dry.

2. Paint the lamp base and any other accent areas black and let them dry.

3. Add black dots with the paint pen, following the lamp's curves and lines.

4. Begin at the base of the lamp with one of the longer lengths of beads, and measure the distance required to make a circle on the base. Cut a length of beads slightly longer than you think you'll need.

5. Use hot glue to attach the beads to the lamp.

6. Trim another length of beads and

glue it on. Continue in this way until you have achieved the desired effect.

Painting the Shade

1. Use dimensional paints on the shade to create neat stacks of painted beads that echo the stacked beads

glued onto the base.

2. Add the fireworks by making flame-like strokes with a brush on dots of paints applied to the upper part of the lamp shade.

3. Screw in the bulb and attach the lamp shade.

Ginger Jar Lamp with Painted Carp

Designer ▪▪ *Cathy Smith*

If you see an oriental-motif lamp in a store, you can expect to pay a high price. But you can make one yourself and be delighted with the results.

What You Need

glazed ceramic or glass lamp in working condition
fine-point black permanent marker
pencil
graphite paper
cellophane tape
black acrylic enamel accent liner paint in an applicator bottle (not the kind that needs baking)
model paint: gloss orange, gold, white, and olive
thinner for model paint
toothpicks
square wire lamp shade frame
heavy white paper
white craft glue
gloss-finish acrylic decoupage compound
orange or red translucent Japanese paper
black satin cord
4 black tassels
finial, Oriental in style
scissors
craft knife
ruler
1-inch (2.5 cm) soft bristle paintbrush

What To Do

Decorating the Base

1. Give the lamp a good cleaning. The surface must be oil-free and dry.

2. Use the marker to draw the fish scale trim on the top and bottom of the lamp.

3. Enlarge the carp patterns on page 74 to the desired size and cut them out, leaving a paper margin around the fish. Lightly tape the pattern onto the graphite paper. Position the graphite paper on the lamp and lightly tape it on. Trace over all the lines with a pencil. When you remove the graphite paper, you will see the transferred design. Finish one side of the lamp at a time.

4. Before you use the accent liner and the model paints, practice using them on a tin can, so you can get the feel of working on a smooth, curved surface.

5. Paint over the outline of the fish with the black accent liner. If you make any mistakes, simply wait until the liner is dry; then cut out any errors with a craft knife and peel them off. You can then correct your outline with fresh paint.

6. Allow the liner to dry and harden (about four hours) before applying the model paint. Use a toothpick to drop enough paint onto the surface of the lamp to make a shallow puddle inside the outlined spaces; then spread the paint with a toothpick to the edge of the outline. Work quickly: within 30 seconds the paint becomes too tacky to spread. Don't try to apply a second coat of model paint. Keep your lamp horizontal, and work from the top to the bottom. Allow each section to dry for 12 hours.

7. Use the marker to draw in water swirls and bubbles around the fish. Outline with the accent liner and let dry completely. Fill in with olive

model paint. Allow the liner to dry for 12 hours.

8. Outline and paint the fish scale trim and let dry.

Making the Shade

1. Measure and then cut out four panels of heavy white paper to fit the four sides of the wire lamp shade frame, adding a ½-inch (1.5 cm) seam allowance for the side, top, and bottom of each panel. Cut out the same amount of Japanese paper.

2. Glue the white paper onto the frame and let it dry.

3. Working quickly (the decoupage compound dries fast), cover half of the outside of one paper panel with decoupage compound and place a panel of Japanese paper on the wet surface. Smooth it down. Repeat this process for the other half of the panel. Use more decoupage compound to glue down the seam allowances. Repeat this process for the other three panels. Allow the shade to dry completely.

4. If you have any bubbles in the rice paper, use the craft knife to make a small slit in the paper. (Don't put a hole in the white paper lining.) Coat the outside of each panel with three coats of decoupage compound, letting the paper dry completely between coats. On the first coat, use the brush to flatten any bubbles.

5. Glue the black satin cord and tassels onto the shade.

6. Screw in the bulb and attach the shade and finial.

Ginger Jar Lamp with Painted Carp

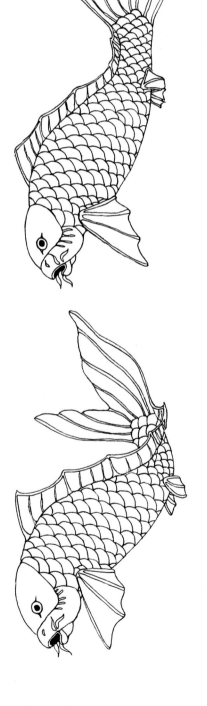

Faux Leopard Skin Chandelier

Designer ■■ *Sheila Ennis Shulz*

With a little fun fabric and some black paint, the designer unleashed the wild side in an otherwise staid chandelier.

What You Need

chandelier in working condition

semi-gloss enamel black spray paint

clip-on lamp shades with self-adhesive backing*

faux animal skin fabric

black cording

white craft glue

light bulbs

measuring tape

scissors

craft knife

*available in most fabric and lamp-supply stores

What To Do

1. Clean the chandelier; then spray it with two coats of black enamel paint, letting each coat dry thoroughly.

2. Measure the fabric you need for the shades and cut it out. Peel off the protective backing on the shades and adhere the fabric to the sticky surface. Trim the fabric, if necessary.

3. Glue on the black cording.

4. Screw in the light bulbs and clip on the shades.

Making Lamps From Traditional and Uncommon Materials

In this section you will find lamps and shades made from a wide assortment of materials, including Japanese rice paper, lumbered and unlumbered wood, gourds, copper tubing, paper mache, glass beads, bamboo, and PVC pipe. As any good cook knows, the right touch with the right technique makes the difference between fast-food fare and gourmet delights. We think the lamps shown here are sensational, combining traditional and uncommon materials, in innovative and appealing ways.

Kyoto Hanging Lantern

Designer ▪▪ Diane Weaver

Clean, spare lines, pleasing shapes, and translucent light give this lamp a distinctly Oriental style, a look that works beautifully with many home decors, from traditional to contemporary.

What You Need

2 pieces of vinyl-coated hardware cloth with a $\frac{5}{8}$-inch (1.75 cm) grid, (1) 12 x 24 inches (30 x 60 cm) and (1) $\frac{5}{8}$ x 32 inches (1.75 x 80 cm)

(2) 11-inch-diameter (28 cm) plastic cake plates with 3 short legs and pleated edges*

6 sheets of handmade paper, each about 30 x 40 inches (75 x 100 cm)

plastic ceiling light fixture, 8 inches (20 cm) in diameter

24 inches of 10-gauge wire

lamp parts with 4$\frac{1}{2}$ inch (11 cm) piece of $\frac{3}{8}$-inch (9 mm) threaded rod, 1$\frac{1}{2}$-inch (4 cm) brass plate, $\frac{3}{8}$-inch (9 mm) and threaded washer and nut

lamp shade top ring, 6 inches (15 cm) in diameter, used with a finial

ceiling plate

8 rubber grommets, 4 for a $\frac{1}{4}$-inch (6 mm) hole, and 4 for a $\frac{1}{8}$-inch (3 mm) hole

spool of 18-gauge wire

plastic wrap

masking tape

fabric stiffener

super-strength modeling polymer

10 wood screw, 2$\frac{1}{2}$ inches (6 cm) long

acrylic paint in black, turquoise, silver, and dark green

gold composite foil and adhesive

super glue

needle-nose pliers

wire cutters

1-inch (2.5 cm) paintbrush

paper clips

spray bottle

*available at party-supply stores or where cake-decorating supplies are sold

What You Do

Making the Cylinder

1. Cut an 8 x 24-inch (20 x 60 cm) piece of hardware cloth and form it into an 8-inch-diameter cylinder. Cut all the little wire ends as close as possible to the horizontal or vertical wire, then wire the two edges together with 18-gauge wire.

2. Cut two sheets of handmade paper slightly larger than the cylinder, and glue them to the cylinder, one sheet at a time. Wrap the paper around the end circumference wires and neatly overlap the paper at the seam.

3. Form a 2-$\frac{1}{2}$ wide x 8-inch high (6 x 20 cm) cylinder with the remaining section of hardware cloth. Trim all but four of the ends off the wire top and bottom. These four ends should be equally spaced around the cylinder—eight $\frac{5}{8}$-inch (1.75 cm) extensions in all.

Decorating the Half Sphere

1. Tightly cover the outside of the plastic sphere in plastic wrap, and secure it with tape.

2. Tear one sheet of paper into triangular strips and cover the plastic half-sphere, using the fabric stiffener to adhere the paper to the plastic. Apply five layers of paper and stiffener, moving around the sphere one layer at a time. Allow the paper to dry for several days before removing it from the plastic.

3. Randomly paint small squares, triangles, trapezoids, circles, and rectangles of adhesive foil on the half-sphere. Then apply the gold foil on these shapes.

4. Cut a hole the size of the wood screw shank in the bottom center of the half-sphere of paper. Using the polymer clay, make a few beads, twist them onto the screw, and bake according to the package directions. Put the screw through a washer, then through the hole in the sphere, through a 1-$\frac{1}{2}$-inch (2 cm) brass plate, and then carefully twist on the clay beads, gluing them in place.

Making the Disks

1. Neatly paint the pleated edges of the cake plates black, inside and out. Let dry.

2. Paint the outside edges with foil adhesive, and, when the adhesive dries, apply the foil.

3. Using the fabric stiffener, apply two layers of paper to one of the plates on the top side, meeting the gilded edge, but leave uncovered a 6-inch-diameter (15 cm) circle in the center of the plate.

4. Press the large paper-covered cylinder into the plate and add another layer of paper and stiffener onto the plate so that the paper comes $\frac{1}{8}$-inch (3 mm) up the cylinder, inside and out, to join the cylinder to the plate. Repeat this procedure with the second plate and the paper half-sphere.

Kyoto Hanging Lantern

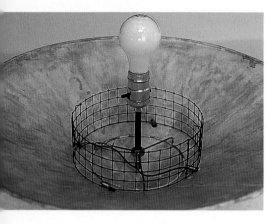

5. Form the ⅝ x 32-inch (1.75x80cm) strip of hardware cloth into a circle and wire the ends together. Place this circle on the bottom of the cake plate that is attached to the sphere, and glue the cylinder and cake plate assembly to it.

Making the Shade

1. Follow steps 1 to 4 in Vase with Paper Mache Shade on page 24, making the cone 21 inches (53 cm) wide and 12 inches (30 cm) deep.

2. Tear the handmade paper into triangular strips. Apply a coat of fabric stiffener to the cone, then place a paper strip on a section of the cone, then coat the paper with another layer of stiffener. Proceed in this manner until you have covered the cone with one layer of paper and stiffener. Repeat this process until you have built up four to six layers of stiffened paper, making sure the total number of layers is equal all the way around the cone.

3. When the paper shade has thoroughly dried, remove it from the pattern and turn it upside down in a bucket. Paper clip the wire circle to the inside edge of the shade. Apply two more layers of paper over the wire to attach it to the shade edge, remov-ing the paper clips as you work around the shade.

4. Glue the 6-inch (15 cm) top fitter lamp shade ring near the top of the shade, using a layer of paper and fabric stiffener to hold it in place.

5. Turn the shade over and mark four points 4½ inches (11 cm) down from the top, spaced equally around the shade. Drill ⅛-inch (3 mm) holes at these points and several other holes at random in the upper part of the shade to allow the heat to escape.

6. Paint the shade with a very light wash of turquoise paint and let dry. Dilute the silver paint with water in the spray bottle and spray it on the shade. Let dry.

Assembling the Lamp

1. Drill four ¼-inch (6 mm) holes in the ceiling plate at four points of the compass, equally spaced from the centered hole.

2. Insert the four small grommets into the four fixed holes in the shade and the four large grommets in the holes in the ceiling plate.

3. Determine the distance your lamp will hang from the ceiling. Measure and cut four strands of electrical wire, two slightly longer then the established distance and two longer still to allow for wiring the lamp. Be careful not to kink the wire.

4. Tie knots in the shorter strands at one end. Insert these two strands through the grommets, one on each side of the shade, and through the ceiling plate; then knot the other ends. Make sure the two tied-off wires are the same length.

5. Insert the threaded rod through the center of the lamp shade ring and fix it firmly in place with a nut, as shown in the drawing.

6. Wire the lamp socket by inserting the two remaining wires through the shade, brass nut, and threaded pipe. Wire and attach the socket.

7. Screw in the light bulb.

8. Tape the electrical wire to the spokes of the lamp ring, to hold their position, as shown in the drawing. Measure the length of the electrical current carrying wires to match the other two, slide them through the grommeted holes in the ceiling plate, and knot them to secure. The detail photo above shows the inside of the wired lamp.

9. Insert the four wire ends on the shorter cylinder of hardware cloth through the grommeted holes in the shade, and bend them down the shade. Then bend the four lower wire extensions at a right angle toward the center of the cylinder. Align the seam in the short cylinder with the seam in the tall cylinder. Poke four holes in the paper of the tall cylinder, under the top wire, to correspond to the spacing of the right-angle wire tips. Slip the wires through the holes.

10. Unless you're experienced at wiring lamps to ceiling fixtures, hire an electrician to do the job.

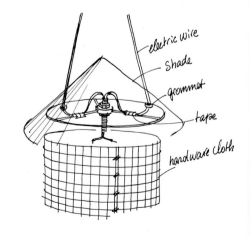

electric wire
shade
grommet
tape
hardware cloth

Tree Lamp

Designer ▪▪ *Pat Scheible*

This rustic floor lamp, simple yet elegant, is made from a sturdy branch that stands alone and needs no further adornment to mark its bold presence.

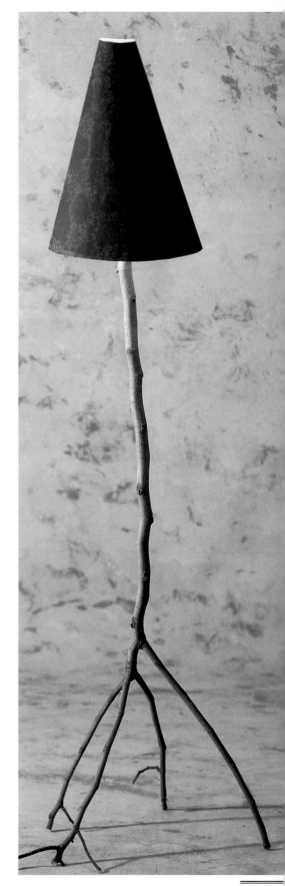

What You Need

sturdy tree branch that will stand up when inverted and trimmed, at least 3 inches (8 cm) in diameter and 4 feet (1.2 m) tall
lamp parts with ⅜-inch (9 mm) threaded rod, socket with side exit for cord
quick-drying epoxy
clip-on top fitter ring
bottom fitter ring
light bulb
wastebasket
decorative paper
craft glue
drill with ⅜-inch (9 mm) bit
heavy pruning shears
scissors

What You Do

Assembling the Base

1. Prune the branch so that it stands steady and secure to a height of about 4 feet (1.2 m)

2. Drill a ⅜-inch (9 mm) wide hole, 1-inch (2.5 cm) deep in the top of the branch, perpendicular to the floor. Screw in the threaded rod, and secure with the washers and nut. Use epoxy for added strength.

3. Attach the socket and lamp cord. Screw in the bulb.

Making the Shade

1. Roll a sheet of decorative paper into a cone shape with the same diameter as the bottom shade ring. Secure the seam with two coats of craft glue.

2. Stand the cone upside down in a wastebasket. Coat the top shade ring with craft glue and set it as far down in the cone as it will go, taking care to keep it aligned with the cone's axis (otherwise the bulb may touch the paper shade). Let the glue dry, then repeat the process with the larger bottom ring.

3. Cut off any excess paper, and clip the shade onto the bulb.

Wrought-Iron Beaded Lamp

Designer ▪▪ *Nancy McGaha*

Sparkling jewels and a simple, wrought-iron base create an alluring lamp. Set it near a window; even when the lamp is switched off, the crystal beads, like little prisms, will catch the sunlight and cast rainbows of light across the room.

What You Need

wrought-iron lamp base*
lamp shade frame, 12 inches (30 cm)
	wide in diameter
spool of 26-gauge gold wire
crystal beads, one color or several
	colors**
other objects that can be strung onto
	wire**
scissors

*sold in many discount stores
**Choose beads that match your decor, or use jewelry pieces from your own collection. The designer used mah-jongg tiles, but you can compose your own theme and add accessories to reflect your tastes and interests.

What You Do

1. Cut dozens of lengths of gold wire, each about 20 to 30 inches (50-75 cm) long.

2. Secure the wire to the lamp shade frame by starting at either the top or bottom of the frame and twisting the wire into place. This is flexible wire and is easy to work with; you can crimp it as you proceed up or down the frame.

3. String the beads or other chosen items onto the wire and allow them to slide around to create the desired effect. Part of the fun in working with this project is watching the wire conform to its own shape as you string the items and let them slide into natural positions. (Tip: If the objects you choose are heavier than crystal beads, you may need to use heavier gauge wire.)

4. Approach the base of the lamp the same way, attaching wire just below the socket, and stringing objects onto the wire.

Paper Mache Floor Lamp with Two Women

Designer ▪▪ *Diane Weaver*

Can you see the two faces? The designer created a unique six-foot floor lamp made of paper mache, supported by a metal and wood armature, then topped with an exquisite handmade shade.

What You Need

(1) ⅜-inch (9 mm) threaded brass rod, 7 inches long (18 cm)

(1) ⅜-inch (9 mm) threaded brass rod, 44 inches long (110 cm)

(3) ⅜-inch (9 mm) nuts

(3) 1-inch (2.5 cm) threaded disks

plastic ceiling replacement fixture, 8 inches (20 cm) in diameter

water putty

plastic bucket

vegetable cooking spray

8-inch (20 cm) disk of heavy cardboard

masking tape

flat black acrylic spray paint

(4) ¾-inch (2 cm) wooden dowels, 36 inches (90 cm) long

(4) #10 wood screws, 2½ (6 cm) long

10 feet (3 m) of ⅜-inch (9 mm) coiled copper tubing

3 feet (90 cm) of ¼-inch (6 mm) copper tubing

(1) 45-degree angle ⅜-inch (9 mm) copper pipe connector

(2) 90-degree-angle ⅜-inch (9 mm) copper pipe connector

(1) T-shaped ⅜-inch (9 mm) copper pipe connector

epoxy made for use with copper plumbing

⅜-inch (9 mm) piece of metal, 2 x 1 inch (5 x 2.5 cm)

spool of 18-gauge wire

spool of 10-gauge wire

plaster impregnated fabric wrap

paper mache pulp

30-inch (75 cm) square of flexible cardboard (not corrugated)

clear, self-adhesive shelf paper

masking tape

large paper clips

large plastic bucket

white handmade paper

fabric stiffener

1 large and 1 medium lamp shade rings

12 feet (4 m) of lamp wire, cord switch, socket, and plug

light bulb

flat black acrylic paint

clear, waterproof, flat sealer

gold metallic acrylic paint

paintbrushes

level

drill with assorted bits

craft knife

pencil

30-inch (75 cm) compass

screwdriver

3-inch-wide (8 cm) paintbrush

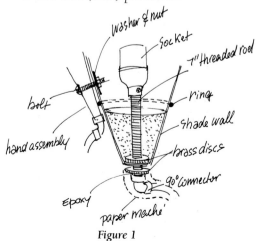

Figure 1

What You Do

Making the Base

1. The lamp base is made from a brass, copper, and wood armature that is wrapped with plaster impregnated fabric wrap and then covered with paper mache pulp. The entire structure sits in a weighted base. To make the weighted base, insert the long threaded rod through the hole in the plastic ceiling fixture and tighten the connection with the washer and nut on the outside, as shown in figure 2 on page 86. Spray the rod and the inside of the plastic half-sphere with vegetable coating. Mix the putty in a bucket, following the manufacturer's directions (it should be the consistency of cake batter) and pour the mold. Tap the mold lightly to bring the air bubbles to the surface. When no more bubbles appear, well before the putty starts to set up, slide the cardboard disk over the rod and tape it to the sides of the mold. Use the level to make sure everything is even. Allow the putty to cure for several hours before you remove the putty base. Spray the weighted base with black paint and let dry.

2. Study figure 2 to make sure you understand the assembly order. The side supports are made from the four 36-inch (90 cm) wooden dowels. Attach the bottom ends of the dowels with wood screws to the two 18-inch arches made from ⅜-inch (9mm) copper tubing. This connection is

Paper Mache Floor Lamp With Two Women

the top center of the arches. Drill holes for the screws through the copper tubing. Drill a center hole through the tubing so you can attach the arched tubes to the threaded rod, using nuts above and below the two tubes, as shown in figure 2.

3. Shave the top ends of the dowels at an angle so they fit securely against the top of the threaded rod. Screw the dowels into position. Tape them in place at the top and then wrap them securely with 18-gauge wire.

4. As shown in figure 2, form the curved arm, shoulder, and head shapes with ⅜-inch (9mm) copper tubing and copper connectors, secured with copper plumbing epoxy. Before gluing the copper pieces together, run the lamp wire through all the pieces; the wire travels up from the half-sphere base, through the long threaded rod, through the 45-degree connector, the first section of the curve that makes a 90-degree turn at the T-connector, and on around to the top of the head, turning again at the right-angle connector, and then out through the short threaded rod.

5. Cover the armature with a good layer of plaster wrap and then a layer of paper mache pulp. Add the curly-Q and other decorative elements, using 10-gauge wire, plaster wrap, and paper mache. For small decorations, simply push them into the drying paper mache. Form the eyes out of paper mache, and let dry. Then attach them to 10-gauge wire with plaster wrap and cover them with more paper mache.

Note: Apply the paper mache pulp by hand and sculpt it by squeezing, pinching, and pushing the wet pulp with your fingers and the palms of your hands. Let the paper mache dry for several days; then spray it black and let dry.

6. Build the hand using ¼ inch (6 mm) coiled copper tubing and the thin piece of metal shaped into a funnel, as shown in figure 3. Cover the hand structure with impregnated plaster wrap and paper mache. Make the bracelet with rolls of paper mache; press them onto the wrist. Let the hand dry. Then paint it black; use the gold paint to color the bracelet. Set the hand aside.

Making the Shade

1. Follow steps 1 to 7 (omitting the small lamp shade ring) in the Vase Lamp with Paper Mache Shade on page 24.

2. Before the last layer of paper is dry, position the two black paper mache rings on the shade. The fabric stiffener will glue them in place, and the damp, glue-covered paper will fill any gaps between the shade and the rings.

Finishing the Lamp

1. Brush a coat of waterproof sealer onto the entire lamp armature, including the hand. Let it dry.

2. When the shade is dry, cut a hole at the top so that the short threaded rod will fit through. Feed a threaded disk onto the top of the short rod and snug it up to the paper mache at the top of the head. Screw or slide the shade into position and then secure it with another disk, as shown in figure 3.

3. Drill a hole in the center of the palm of the hand and slide a short bolt through it. Position the hand on the arm, using a 90-degree copper connector (figure 1, page 84).

4. Cut a small hole in the shade to allow the bolt to come through, and then secure the bolt with a washer and nut, as shown in figure 3. Glue together the copper connector and the hand and arm assembly. Cover the wrist joint and the bolt with plaster wrap and paper mache pulp. When dry, paint it black.

5. Prepare and pour water putty into the bottom of the shade to a depth of 4 inches (10 cm). Let it harden.

6. Wire on the socket, switch, and plug. Screw in the light bulb.

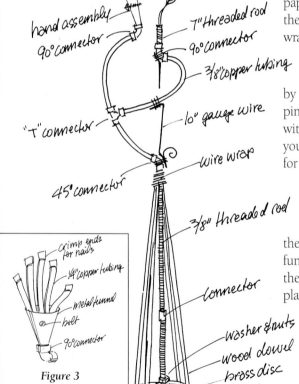

Figure 2

hand assembly
90° connector
7" threaded rod
90° connector
⅜" copper tubing
"T" connector
10" gauge wire
wire wrap
45° connector
⅜" threaded rod
crimp ends for nails
¼" copper tubing
metal funnel
bolt
90° connector
Figure 3
connector
washer & nuts
wood dowel
brass disc
screw
⅜" copper tubing
Base

Gourd Sconce

Designer ▪▪ *Ginger Summit*

Here's a wall sconce with natural beauty, made from a dried gourd, and embellished with dozens of small holes.

What You Need

gourd, cured and clean*
2 scraps of metal, 6 - 12 inches (15 - 31 cm) long
screws
brown leather dye
socket and lamp cord
light bulb
hand or power cutting tool
file
drill with assorted bits
screwdriver

*Gourds can be grown from seed or purchased from garden stores and farmers' markets. Ginger Summit's book The Complete Book of Gourd Craft (Lark Books, 1996) features a source list for purchasing seeds and gourds, as well as instructions for growing and decorating gourds.

What You Do

1. Cut the gourd from the top stem down the side to the bottom. Cut out an opening for the hardware at the center top. File the edges smooth. Scoop out the dried pulp.

2. Bend the metal strips so that you create a top and bottom shelf for the socket and cord to rest on; screw them to the gourd.

3. Make holes with the drill, using an assortment of drill bits to create a random pattern with different sized holes.

4. Stain the gourd with the leather dye.

5. Slip the socket and cord into place. Screw in the light bulb.

Leather-Plaited Gourd

Designer ▪▪ *Ginger Summit*

The designer wove rawhide leather strips onto an unfinished gourd and created a stunning blend of rustic and contemporary that complements many room settings.

What You Need

bottle gourd, cured and clean*

leather lamp shade**

round wooden or ceramic base

sturdy twine

rawhide leather strips (available at leather-supply shops)

rubber bands

metal clamps

wood glue

leather dye, neutral shade (available at shoe stores)

lamp parts; see pages 9-10

wooden bead or miniature gourd for a finial

metal spoon

power or hand cutting tool

file

drill with ⅛-inch (3 mm) and ¼-inch (6 mm) bits

awl

---

*Gourds can be grown from seed or purchased from garden stores and farmers' markets. Ginger Summit's book The Complete Book of Gourd Craft *(Lark Books, 1996) features a source list for purchasing seeds and gourds, as well as instructions for growing gourds and decorating them.*

** Before you start, take the gourd to a lamp shop that sells shades. Choose a shade appropriate in size to the gourd. Deciding on the shade first allows you to know where to cut and trim the gourd for a proper fit.

What You Do

1. Start with a clean gourd. Use the spoon to scrape out any pulp remaining on the inside.

2. Cut the neck of the gourd so it will fit the shade. Cut the base, using the wooden ring as a guide for size and fit. You want the gourd to sit level on the ring so it can stand without wobbling. File the cut edges smooth.

3. Soak the leather strips for one hour in cool water. If the water is too hot the leather will shrink. Soaking allows for more flexibility, making the leather easier to work with.

4. Make a ring of sturdy twine to act as an anchor for the leather strips.

5. Wrap or drape the wet rawhide strips over the ring and then around the neck of the gourd. Hold them in place with rubber bands.

6. Begin plaiting the leather strips—over one, under one—in a simple basket weave pattern. Weave the leather strips the length of the neck, securing them at intervals with rubber bands. Note: It's important to secure the strips with rubber bands or you'll be a basket case yourself trying to keep them from slipping and sliding.

7. Continue weaving around the bulbous part of the lamp base. At the edge of the hole cut into the base, secure the strips with clamps. Adjust the weaving to make sure it's even. As the rawhide dries it will shrink and tighten to the gourd; that's why having the clamps in place is so important.

8. After the strips have dried, remove the clamps. At the site where the hole was cut into the base, you can dab a little wood glue to make sure the strips remain secure.

9. When everything is dry, use the leather dye to completely coat the base.

10. Use the awl to punch tiny holes in the top and bottom edge of the lamp shade. Weave rawhide strips in and out of these holes.

11. Assemble the lamp components and wire the lamp.

12. Screw in the bulb and attach the shade and finial.

Shaker–Style Table Lamp

Designer ▪▪ *Sheila Ennis Schulz*

Reminiscent of the classic lines in Shaker furnishings, this design uses painted PVC pipe as the base, a distinctive shade, and an ornate brass finial. The result adds credence to the "less is more" school of thought.

What You Need

1¾-inch (4.5 cm) PVC pipe, 13 inches (33.5 cm) long*

acrylic spray paint in pale green and brownish red

round wooden lamp base, 3-4 inches (8-10 cm) in diameter

glazing medium with dark brown tint

sponges

lamp parts; see pages 9-10

vase cap

light bulb

lamp shade with simulated reddish brown wood veneer

brass finial

drill with assorted bits

*Most hardware and building-supply stores will cut the pipe to your specifications.

What You Do

1. Spray the PVC pipe with light green paint. Apply several coats, allowing the paint to dry in between each coat.

2. Drill a hole through the center of the round wooden base to accommodate the threaded rod and cord.

3. Spray the wooden base with red paint, applying several coats. Allow it to dry.

4. Glaze the wooden base, sponging on the dark brown tint.

5. Assemble the lamp parts and wire the lamp, placing the PVC pipe over the wooden base. Attach the vase cap.

6. Screw in the light bulb and attach the shade and finial.

Chessa's Dream

Designer ▪▪ *Pat Schieble*

A dream-come-true for that special cheerleader, this charming lamp is easy to make (and when the light is turned on, the heat causes the pom-poms to wave.) You can make other lamps like it, using other types of trophies—golf, wrestling, or sailing.

What You Need

old pleated lamp shade or new shade

pink boa (available at toy stores)

iridescent plastic gift wrap

spray adhesive

craft glue

cheerleader trophy

cyanoacrylate glue

wooden yarn spindle, or wooded
 dowel, or pvc pipe

and a wooden disk

wood glue (optional)

all-purpose latex primer

white acrylic paint

glitter

lamp parts; see pages 9-10

light bulb

scissors

paintbrush

drill with assorted bits

What You Do

1. Old pleated lamp shades, often found at yard sales, can be easily taken apart. The pleated material is glued at the top and bottom, and it's easy to pop it loose. The shade liner is sturdy, translucent, and flameproof, just begging for a new look. Or, you can buy a new shade and embellish it as described here. Simply spray the liner with adhesive and cover it with the gift wrap; wrinkles are just fine.

2. Use craft glue to attach bands of boa to the top and bottom of the shade. Glue puffs of the boa onto the cheerleader's hands.

3. Clean and prime the spindle, or whatever you're using for the stem and base of the lamp. If you are making the base, glue the base to the wooden or plastic stem. When dry, apply two coats of white paint, sprinkling glitter into the last coat before the paint dries.

4. Use the cyanoacrylate glue to attach the trophy to the top lamp shade ring.

5. Wire the lamp. Screw in the light bulb and attach the shade.

The Reader's Lamp

Designer ▪▪ *Diane Weaver*

With its spectacled book lover suspended from the pull chain, this whimsical lamp casts the perfect mood and light for a much-needed night of reading.

What You Need

½ inch (1.5 cm) copper pipe, 20 inches (50 cm) long

lamp parts with ⅜ inch (9 mm) threaded rod and pull chain; see pages 9-10

plastic ceiling replacement fixture, 8 inches (20 cm) in diameter

(2) small plastic buckets, about 6 inches (15 cm) wide

plasticine modeling clay

vegetable cooking spray

water putty

super-strength modeling polymer

8-inch (20 cm) disk of heavy cardboard

masking tape

acrylic craft paints

cyanoacrylate glue

clear acrylic spray sealer

wooden disk, 1 x 9½ inches (2.5 x 24 cm)

(3) rubber bumpers, 3½ inches (9 cm) high

white lamp shade

light bulb

level

paintbrushes

drill with ⅜ -inch (9 mm) bit

steel wool

Figure 1

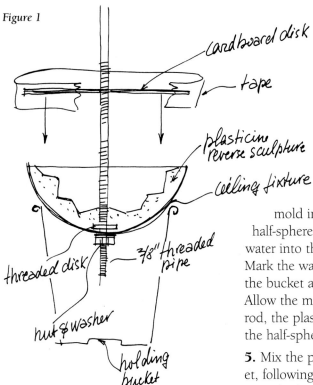

cardboard disk

tape

plasticine reverse sculpture

ceiling fixture

threaded disk

3/8" threaded pipe

nut & washer

holding bucket

What You Do

Preparing the Mold

1. As shown in figure 1, turn the threaded disk onto the threaded rod, insert the rod through the hole in the plastic ceiling fixture (this is your mold), and tighten the connection with the nut on the outside. Allow the rod to extend only slightly past the nut.

2. Place this assembly on one of the plastic buckets, as shown in figure 1, and check to see if the rod is perpendicular to the imaginary diametric plane of the sphere.

3. Mold the plasticine to form the negative areas of the sofas and tables; size this to fit inside the half-sphere. If you have a difficult time visualizing what this shape should look like, first make a miniature model of one sofa and table out of plasticine. Study the negative areas, imagining them inside

a sphere, and then proceed with your negative mold. A long rectangle of clay forms the book shelf. Press the plasticine into the plastic half-sphere.

4. To measure how much putty you will need to fill the mold in one pouring, fill the half-sphere with water and pour the water into the other plastic bucket. Mark the water depth on the side of the bucket and discard the water. Allow the mold to dry. Then spray the rod, the plasticine, and the inside of the half-sphere with vegetable coating.

5. Mix the putty in the marked bucket, following the manufacturer's directions (it should be the consistency of cake batter), and pour the mold. Tap the mold lightly with your hands to bring the air bubbles to the surface of the putty. When no more bubbles appear, well before the putty starts to set up, slide the cardboard disk over the rod (see figure 1), and tape it to the sides of the mold. Then use the level to make sure everything is as you intend. Allow the putty to cure for several hours before you remove the putty base.

Finishing the Lamp

1. Allow the unmolded base to air dry for a few days. Temporarily remove the rod by unscrewing it from the base. Then paint the base as desired with the acrylic paints.

2. Make the books from the super-strength modeling polymer and fire them according to the manufacturer's directions. Then paint the books. Arrange them on the base and glue them in place.

3. Drill a 3/8-inch (9 mm) hole in the center of the wooden disk, as shown in figure 2. Sand the disk and paint it. Let it dry; then glue it to the painted plasticine base.

4. Buff the copper rod with steel wool, and spray it with an acrylic sealer.

5. Glue the bumpers to the bottom of the wooden base.

6. Paint the shade with broad strokes and let it dry.

7. Assemble the lamp parts and wire the lamp.

8. Screw in the light bulb and attach the shade and finial.

1/2 copper tubing

3/8" threaded pipe

sculpture

wood base

bumpers

washer

nut

Figure 2

Fabric Canister

Designer ▪▪ *Sheila Ennis Schulz*

It's hard to believe that this sophisticated lamp is made from heavy-duty PVC pipe. The well-chosen fabric and shade give it a classic look.

What You Need

upholstery fabric of your choice
4-inch-diameter (10.5 cm) PVC pipe, 13 inches (33.5 cm) long
black spray paint
wooden lamp base
wood glue
4 wooden balls
translucent black paper shade
lamp parts; see pages 9-10
vase cap to match the pipe size
brass or gold finial
light bulb
scissors
sewing machine

What You Do

1. Cut the fabric to fit the pipe, leaving room for a ⅝-inch (1.75 cm) seam allowance.

2. Sew the fabric sleeve to fit the pipe. You'll want a nice, snug fit.

3. Spray the wooden lamp base and the wooden balls with black paint and let dry.

4. Glue the balls to the base.

5. Assemble the lamp components and wire the lamp, setting the PVC pipe over the base. Attach the vase cap.

6. Screw in the light bulb and attach the shade and finial.

Autumn Leaf Luminator

Designer ▪▪ *Ellen Zahorec*

Bring a little nature into your home with this charming accent lamp, or decorate it with other special items, such as lace or handmade paper.

What You Need

self-adhesive luminator lamp*

flat items, such as dried or silk leaves and flowers, pieces of lace, or decorative papers

several sheets of tissue, rice, or lace paper

acrylic polyurethane or decoupage medium

60-watt bulb

scissors

paintbrush

*Lamps such as this one can be ordered through mail-order suppliers. See the Supplier List on page 142.

What You Do

1. Remove the protective paper on the lamp. Adhere the leaves or other flat objects to the sticky surface.

2. Measure the tissue, rice, or lace paper to a size that will wrap around the lamp, leaving ½ inch (1.5 cm) extra in length where the seams will meet. Cut the paper and place it on top of the leaves; don't worry about wrinkles.

3. Coat the paper with acrylic polyurethane or a decoupage medium. This will smooth out any wrinkles and give the lamp a translucent look even when the lamp is turned off.

4. Screw in the bulb.

Walnut Floor Lamp

Designer ▪▪ *Mark Strom*

This striking lamp highlights the rich appeal of wood, with its clean, simple, yet commanding lines.

Cut List

walnut:

(2) 50¼ x 3 x 1½ inches
   (129 x 7.5 x 4 cm)
(4) 5 x 4 x ¾ inches (13 x 10.5 x 2 cm)
(4) 47 x 1½ x ¾ inches
   (12 x 4 x 2 cm)
(1) 4¾ x 4¾ x ¾ inches
   (12.5 x 12.5 x 2 cm)

What You Need

piece of cardboard, 47 x 6 inches
   (121 x 15 cm)
(4)   #8 x 1¼-inch (3.5 cm) screws
(12) 8 x 2-inch (6.5 cm) screws
(8)   ⅜ inch-diameter (9 mm)
   button-type screw plugs
wood glue
clear lacquer
lamp parts; see pages 9-10
1-inch (2.5 cm) brads
harp-style lamp shade, 24-30-inch
   (62-77 cm) diameter
router with ⅜-inch (9 mm) round over
   bit and ⅜-inch (9 mm) cove bit
table saw
6 clamps with 6-inch (15.5 cm) openings
block plane
cutting knife
white chalk

fine-bladed saber saw
150-grit sandpaper
drill with ⅜-inch (9 mm) bit and #8
   countersink
paintbrush

What You Do

1. Using the table saw or router with a straight bit, cut a slot ¾ x ¾ inch (2 x 2 cm) down the center of both of the 50¼-inch-long (129 cm) pieces on one of their 3-inch (7.5 cm) sides.

2. Carefully line up all edges and ends. Then glue the two pieces together. Let the pieces sit for a few minutes; then clamp them together while the glue dries. Pausing before you clamp reduces some of the movement when the clamps are tightened. The better the edges are aligned and the cleaner the glue up, the easier it will be to clean up and sand the pieces.

3. Glue one 5 x 4 x ¾-inch (13 x 10.5 x 2 cm) piece to one end of each piece that measures 47 inches (121 cm) long, as shown in figure 1. Make sure the alignment is as clean as possible.

Figure 1

4. Using the block plane, clean up and level all glue lines.

5. On the piece of cardboard, draw the pattern for the side legs (see figures 2 and 3.) Note: This cut must be identical on each piece. Basic measurements are given in figure 2. The curves can be drawn according to your preference, but they must all be cut the same so the effect is the same.

6. Cut the pattern out, being careful to make straight, clean cuts.

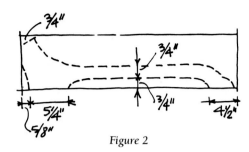

Figure 2

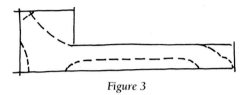

Figure 3

7. Transfer and mark the pattern on each 47-inch-long (121 cm) piece.

8. Using the finest blade saber saw (in order to get the cleanest cut), follow the pattern lines in cutting each piece. The cleaner and slower the cuts, the more accurate each piece will be. Note: The bottom cuts must be identical or the lamp will not stand level when the legs are attached.

9. Smooth all saber saw cuts with 150-grit sandpaper. Round all edges with a router that has a ⅜-inch (9 mm) round over bit. Round all the edges, except the inside one on the top and bottom of each leg, as shown in figure 4. These are the edges that sit against the central post of the lamp.

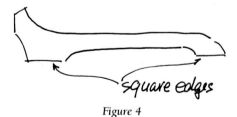

Figure 4

10. Round all four edges of the 50-inch long (129 cm) post.

11. Using the router with the ⅜-inch (9 mm) cove bit, route a coved edge on all four edges on both sides of the piece that measures 4¾ x 4¾ x ¾ inches (12.5 x 12.5 x 2 cm.) Set the router to leave a ¼-inch-square (6 mm) edge in the center of the piece (see figure 5.)

Figure 5

12. Find the center of the 4¾ inch (12.5 cm) square, and drill a ⅜-inch-diameter (9 mm) hole through the piece. This is for the lamp hardware.

13. Line up the four 47-inch-long (121 cm) pieces; these are the four side legs. Align the ends.

14. Using a drill with a #8 counter-sink, drill two countersunk holes through each piece on each end, making sure all the holes line up (see figure 6). Note: These holes should be drilled to line up with the flat areas that will attach to the lamp base, as shown in figure 7.

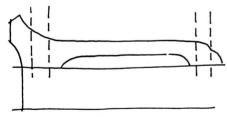

Figure 6

Figure 7

15. Sand all the pieces on all sides with the 150-grit sandpaper.

16. Center the 47-inch-long (121 cm) side leg on the side of the lamp post, making sure the curved cut on the bottom is flush with the bottom of the post. Note: This is critical for a

Walnut Floor Lamp

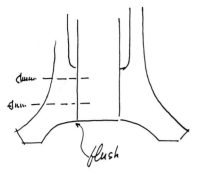

Figure 8

level and stable lamp (see figure 8).

17. Predrill the hole and attach one leg, starting at the top with a #8 x 1-¼-inch (3.5 cm) screw. For the remaining holes, use the #8 x 2½ inch (6.5 cm) screws.

18. Repeat this process with the other three legs. Glue and plug all the screw holes with the ⅜-inch (9 mm) wood buttons.

19. Apply a finish of clear lacquer and let it dry.

20. Feed the lamp cord through the bottom of the lamp base. Attach the lamp components to the 4¾-inch (12.5 cm) square.

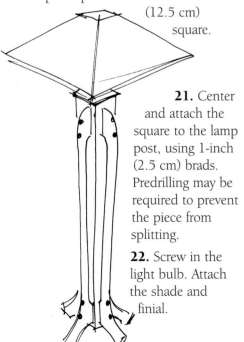

21. Center and attach the square to the lamp post, using 1-inch (2.5 cm) brads. Predrilling may be required to prevent the piece from splitting.

22. Screw in the light bulb. Attach the shade and finial.

Copper Gourd

Designer ▪▪ *Ginger Summit*

This gorgeous gourd table lamp features the motifs and shimmering colors of a sunny autumn day.

What You Need

hardshell, short-handled dipper gourd, cured and cleaned*

acrylic metallic paint, antique copper, and 2 or 3 darker, complementary colors

assorted dry leaves

netting cord (available in craft- and basketry-supply stores)

wooden ring for base of lamp, sized to fit the bottom of the gourd

spool of thin-gauge copper wire

monofilament

translucent paper lamp shade**

polyurethane stain

lamp parts; see pages 9-10

light bulb

paintbrush

power or hand cutting tool

metal spoon

file

drill with ⅛-inch (3 mm) and ¼-inch (6 mm) bits

*Gourds can be grown from seed or purchased from garden stores and farmers' markets. Ginger Summit's book The Complete Book of Gourd Craft *(Lark Books, 1996) features a source list for purchasing seeds and gourds, as well as instructions for growing gourds and decorating them.*

** Before you start, take the gourd to a lamp shop that sells shades. Choose a shade appropriate in size to the gourd. Deciding on the shade first allows you to know where to cut and trim the gourd for a proper fit.

What You Do

1. Start with a clean gourd. Use a spoon to scrape out any pulp remaining on the inside. Cut and trim the gourd at the neck to fit the lamp shade and lamp components. File the cut edges smooth.

2. Apply a base coat of copper paint to the gourd and allow it to dry completely.

3. Print a leaf pattern on the gourd using the dried leaves and the darker metallic paint.

4. Wrap the netting cord around the neck of the gourd in a knotless netting design, pulling each strand taut. It should stay in place without gluing. Note: Detailed instructions for knotless netting appear in many basketry and handweaving books. Basically, it involves working in a circle with the cord, creating a spiral web pattern. You will need to drill a hole in the gourd and stitch the cord at the area where the first row of netting will be anchored. After sewing on this line, begin to make loops. You'll need to drill another small hole to anchor the end of the cord.

5. Paint the wooden ring with copper paint and let dry. Then wrap the wooden ring with copper wire.

6. Drill ⅛-inch (3 mm) holes in the bottom of the gourd.

7. Secure the wrapped wooden ring to the gourd base with monofilament, threading the line in and out of the drilled holes.

8. Paint the rings of knotless netting with metallic paint.

9. Imprint the shade with a leaf pattern.

10. Apply a thin coat of polyurethane to the gourd and the shade to give the lamp extra shine and protection.

11. Wire the lamp. Screw in the bulb and attach the shade and finial.

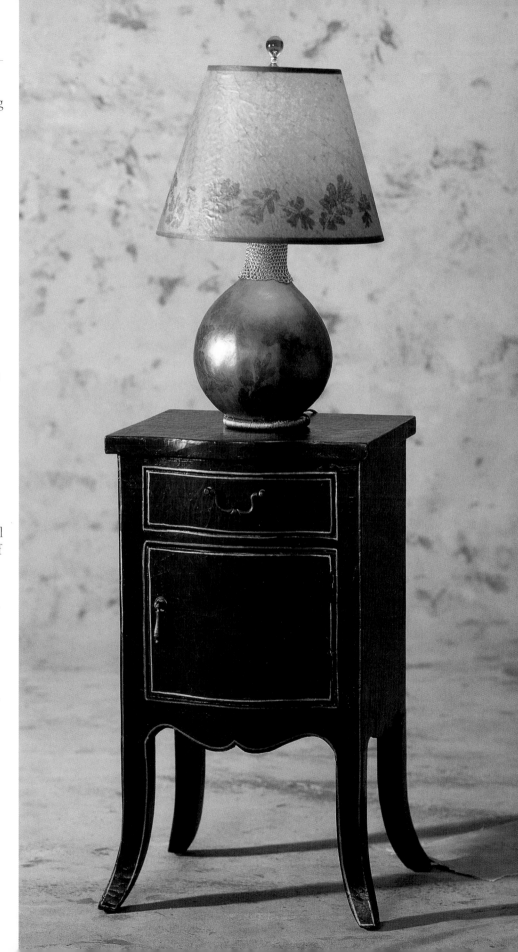

CD Cabinet Floor Lamp

Designer ▪▪ *Peggy Hayes*

An inventive blend of practicality and style, this charming storage unit with a built-in lamp can be used in any room.

Cut List

1-inch (2.5 cm) pine:
(2) sides : 7⅛ inches x 4 feet (18.32 cm x 1.24 m)
(1) shelf A: 6 x 7⅛ inches (15.5 x 18.32 cm)
(6) shelf B* : 6 x 6¼ inches (15.5 x 16 cm)
(2) brace A : ¾ x 4¾ inches (2 x 12 cm)
(2) brace B : 3/4 x 6 inches (2 x 15.5 cm)
(2) wedges : 7½ x 3½ inches (19 x 9 cm). Leaving 7½ inches (19 cm) across the bottom, cut a 45-degree angle on both sides up to a height of 3½ inches (9 cm).
(1) roof A : 6¾ x 9¼ inches (17.5 x 24 cm)
(1) roof B: 7½ x 9¼ inches (19 x 24 cm)
(1) door: 5-¾ x 3-¾ inches (14 x 9 cm)
(1) platform: 11¼ x 11-¼ inches (29 x 29 cm)
2-inch (5.5 cm) pine:
(1) chimney: 2 x 4¼ inches (5.5 x 11 cm)
½-inch (1.5 cm) plywood:
(1) back: 7⅜ x 3⅞ inches (18.95 x 9.7 cm)

What You Need

1-inch (2.5 cm) screws
2-inch (5 cm) wreath
(4) miniature wooden triangles
(2) miniature wooden door posts
wooden cabinet handle
(2) hinges, 1½ x ⅞ inch (4 x 2.4 cm)
cabinet magnet with plate
wood filler
sandpaper
wood glue
paintbrushes: ¾ inch (2 cm), ⅜ inch (9 mm), ¼ inch (6 mm)
paint pens, white and black
acrylic paints in colors of your choice
acrylic gloss varnish
13-inch (33.5 cm) white fabric shade
lamp parts with 6- to 8-inch (15-20 cm) assembly rod; see pages 9-10
small brads
bench saw
drill with ⅛-inch (3 mm), ⅜-inch (9 mm), ¼-inch (6 mm), and ½-inch (1.5 cm) bits
screwdriver
hammer

What You Do

Building the Cabinet

1. Cut the wood as indicated in the Cut List.

2. Sand all the pieces.

3. Drill ⅛-inch (3 mm) pilot holes for the screws; then drill ⅜-inch (9 mm) holes to countersink the screws.

4. Screw the sides to bottom shelf A. Make sure the shelf is flush with the sides in front and back.

5. Screw the sides to shelf B.

6. Screw brace A parts even with the top of each side. They will be recessed evenly from front and back.

7. Screw brace B parts across the front and back, between the sides, to brace A parts.

8. Screw the wedges to the B braces.

9. Screw roof A to the front and back wedges.

10. Screw roof B to roof A and to the front and back wedges. Be sure roof B overlaps roof A at the top, as shown in the drawing on page 102.

11. To secure the platform, center the cabinet on the platform and screw through the bottom shelf.

12. Drill a ½-inch (1.5 cm) hole lengthwise through the center of the chimney piece, as shown in the drawing.

13. Cut a 45-degree angle in the chimney piece, ½ inch (1.5 cm) from the

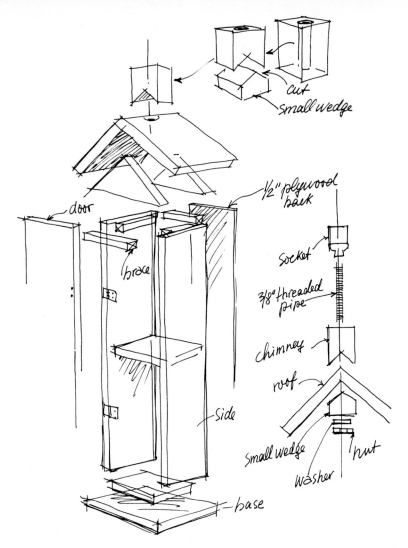

cut
small wedge

1/2" plywood back

door

brace

socket

3/8" threaded pipe

chimney

side

roof

small wedge

nut

washer

base

shade. Paint the top and bottom trim. Don't thin the paint.

Finishing and Wiring the Lamp

1. Drill a ¼-inch (6 mm) hole through the back wedge.

2. Thread the assembly rod through the chimney, roof, and small wedge. Thread the lamp cord through the ¼-inch (6 mm) hole in back, through the nut, washer, and into the rod, as shown in the drawing.

3. Complete the wiring.

Finishing the Cabinet

1. Attach the door to the front of the cabinet with hinges.

2. Attach the plywood back with small brads.

3. Attach the handle to the door.

4. Mount the magnet inside the cabinet, making sure you recess it ¾ inch (2 cm) so that when the door is closed the corresponding plate (to be attached in step 5) will strike the magnet.

5. Mount the magnet plate on the inside of the cabinet door. Make sure it hits the magnet when the door closes.

bottom. Save the small wedges: you will use these when wiring the lamp.

14. Attach the chimney to the center of the roof using wood glue. Allow it to dry thoroughly.

15. Using the hole in the glued chimney as a guide, drill a ½-inch (1.5 cm) hole through the roof.

16. Fill the screw holes with filler; when dry, sand.

Painting and Decorating the Cabinet and Lamp Shade

1. Prime the cabinet, door, and plywood back of the cabinet.

2. Paint the cabinet, door, and back of the unit.

3. Paint the door, platform, and chimney, using the project photograph as a guide. Use the white paint pen to trim around the windows and door, and to draw mortar lines on the porch and chimney. Use the black pen to paint the light and the light post.

4. Apply a light coat of varnish to the entire cabinet and allow to dry.

5. Paint the wooden triangles and the front door posts with the colors of your choice. When dry, glue the triangles to the cabinet door. Glue one set of triangles under the roof peak.

6. Paint the lamp shade by mixing three parts paint and one part water, letting the background colors blend together. Allow to dry.

7. Paint clouds and birds on the lamp

A Lamp Named Bob

Designer ▪▪ ■ *Pat Scheible*

Bob once did double duty as part of a dishwasher kit. Now reborn into a campy lamp, he's a cool and flexible guy. A little push sets him bobbing— hence the name. (The dog's name is Golda.)

What You Need

copper tubing from a dishwasher hook-up kit
weight from a floor-lamp base*
keyless porcelain socket
lamp parts with (2) ⅜-inch (9 mm) threaded rods, (1) 6 inches (15.5 cm) long, (1) 3 inches (7.5 cm) long; see pages 9-10
flared lamp fitting
25-watt globe bulb
epoxy

*Inside almost every faux brass floor lamp is a black weight waiting to be discovered and displayed. Look for old lamps at flea markets or check around the house for discards.

What You Do

1. Straighten the copper tubing and push the lamp cord through.

2. Attach the 6-inch (15.5 cm) rod to the base with washers and nuts. Thread one end of the cord through the pipe.

3. Slip a nut, washer, 3-inch (7.5 cm) rod, and socket over the other end of the cord. Attach the socket and tighten up everything.

4. Mix a generous quantity of epoxy and slather it on the pipes. Slip the ends of the copper tubing over the pipes and allow it to harden.

5. Add the plug and screw in the bulb.

6. Twist the copper tubing into any configuration. Give it a little push and watch the lamp bob!

Corrugated Lantern

Designer ▪▪ *Pamella Wilson*

The architectural lines of this design evoke the look of a building with many windows and an open tower roof. Yet this handsome miniature is made from modest and inexpensive materials.

What You Need

sheet of corrugated cardboard, 24 x 12 inches (60 x 30 cm)

(14) mini-blind slats, 15 inches (38 cm) long

gold spray paint

small table lamp (see figure 3)

light bulb

craft glue

cutting mat

metal ruler, about 1¼ inches (3.5 cm) wide

pencil

craft knife

What You Do

1. On the flat side of the cardboard, mark vertical lines along the length. Use the width of the ruler for a spacer.

2. To create a checkerboard effect, mark horizontal lines on the cardboard, using the ruler as a spacer (see figure 1).

3. Cut horizontal slits in the cardboard, alternating columns. Repeat this procedure all the way down the sheet. Leave an uncut margin on both sides, as shown in the drawing.

4. In a similar manner, cut through the uncut rows, but start with the ruler halfway down one square, so that the slits fall halfway between the first ones you cut.

5. Spray paint the front and back of the cardboard, and let dry.

6. Weave the mini-blind slats through the cardboard slits, allowing about 1 inch (2.5 cm) to protrude as shown in figure 1.

7. With the corrugated side facing out, form a cylindrical shape. Trim the edges so there is little overlapping, as shown in figure 3. Glue the edges together and let dry.

8. Screw in the bulb. Place the lantern on top of the table lamp.

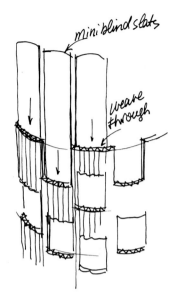

Figure 2

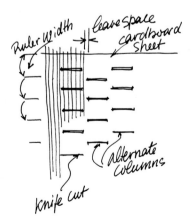

Figure 1

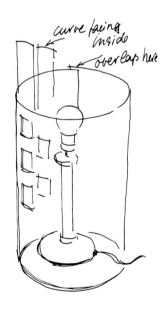

Figure 3

Free-form Lantern

Designer ▪▪ *Pamella Wilson*

This unusual lamp combines the soft light of Christmas bulbs, delicate-looking handmade paper, and a flexible wire structure. The result is a free-form design that creates a lovely mood.

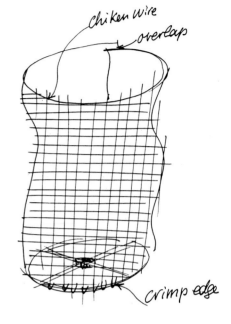

Figure 1

What You Need

lamp shade frame, at least 3 x 4 feet
  (.9 x 1.2 m)
length of chicken wire, at least 4 feet
  (1.3 m) long*
fencing wire, enough to form several U-
  shaped pins*
thick leather gloves
tissue paper
dried leaves, decorative paper, scraps of
  greeting cards (see step 6)
string of 50 small white Christmas lights
water-based varnish
pair of pliers
paintbrush

*available at hardware or building-supply
stores

What You Do

1. Turn the lamp shade frame upside down so you can use the top as a base. Bend the chicken wire around the hoop to create a large cylinder, crimping the edge closed with pliers, as shown in figure 1. You'll need to wear your leather gloves while bending the wire.

2. Cut off the excess wire. Bend the edges together to make a seam.

3. Form U-shaped pins with 3-inch (8 cm) pieces of fencing wire.

4. Attach the string of white lights to the inside of the cylinder, using the U-pins (see figure 2).

5. Bend and twist the cylinder into whatever form you desire.

6. Cover the wire with small pieces of tissue paper, brushing over with generous amounts of varnish. You can add dried leaves, pieces of favorite greeting cards, decorative wrapping paper, or other bits of paper memorabilia. Repeat the process until you have covered the wire with at least four layers of paper.

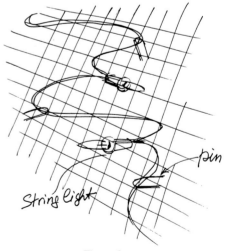

Figure 2

Cypress Lamp

Designer ▪▪ *Mark Strom*

The natural beauty of wood is elegantly displayed in this appealing design. Coved edging on the base gives it an interesting "lift" but also allows for attaching the base to a table or other piece of furniture.

C u t   L i s t

cypress:
(2) 9-½ x 3-¾ x 1-⅜ inch (24.5 x 9.5 x 5 cm)
(2) 9-½ x 1-⅜ x 1-⅜ inch (24.5 x 5 x 5 cm)
(1) 3 x 3 x ¾ inch (8 x 8 x 2 cm)
(1) 3-⅜ x 3-⅜ x ¾ inch (9 x 9 x 2 cm)
(12) 3-¾ x ½ x 1/2 inch (9.5 x 1.5 x 1.5 cm)

What You Need

piece of cork

lamp parts; see pages 9-10

lamp shade

clear lacquer

wood glue

sandpaper

nail set

rule

table saw

miter box and saw

router with ⅜-inch (9 mm) cove bit

1-inch (2.5 cm) brads

hammer

drill with ¼-inch (6 mm) and ⅜-inch
    (9 mm) bits

straight slot screwdriver

What You Do

1. Cut the wood pieces to the dimensions listed.

2. Glue the two 9½ x 1⅜ x 1⅜-inch pieces (24.5 x 5 x 5 cm) to the face of a 9½ x 3¾ x 1⅜-inch piece (24.5 x 9.5 x 5 cm). Line up the outside edges and ends as shown in figure 1. Allow the glued pieces to set. This helps prevent the pieces from moving around when they are clamped in place. When set, clamp together, making sure all the outside edges are square. Let dry.

3. Repeat the process, gluing the 9½ x 3¾ x 1⅜-inch piece (24.5 x 9.5 x 5 cm) to the top of the first glued piece in order to form a box. (See figure 2.) Allow the glue to dry.

4. Now you are ready to rout all the edges. Using a router with a ⅜-inch (9 mm) cove bit, rout the edges on one face of both the 3-inch (8 cm) square and the 3⅜-inch (9 cm) square. Set the router depth to leave a ⅜-inch (9 mm) edge. Place the wood on a non-skid surface (here's where a piece of cork comes in handy) to prevent the square from shifting during the routing process.

5. Locate the center of the 3 x 3 x ¾-inch piece (8 x 8 x 2 cm.) Drill a ⅜-inch-diameter (9 mm) hole for the threaded rod to pass through.

6. Miter cut the 12 small pieces from short point to short point. Measure down ⅛ inch (3 mm) from the top end of the square and attach the first mitered piece with glue. You'll find that gluing is slower during this part of the project because you must wait for one side to dry before moving onto the next side. However, your patience will be rewarded with a more polished-looking lamp. Measure down ⁷⁄16 inch and add another mitered piece. Repeat this process for the third piece. Repeat the entire procedure on the other three sides.

7. Drill a ¼-inch (6 mm) hole through the bottom side of the lamp box for the lamp cord to pass through, as shown in figure 2.

8. Sand all the pieces.

9. Apply a coat or two of clear lacquer to all the pieces.

10. Run the lamp cord through the ¼-inch (6 mm) hole and through the top of the box. Completing this step now is easier than doing it after assembling all the pieces.

11. Center the 3⅜-inch (9 cm) square—keeping the coved side facing out—onto the base of the lamp. Attach this square using 1-inch (2.5 cm) brads. If you like, you can predrill the nail holes.

12. Attach the lighting components to the 3-inch-square (8 cm) piece. Then attach this square to the top of the lamp using the same methods as described in step 11.

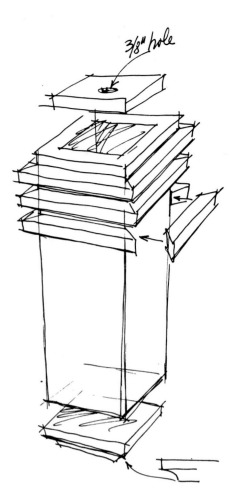

Figure 1

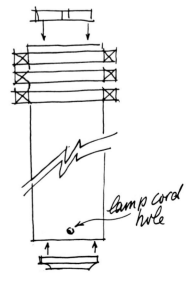

Figure 2

Fallen Wood Lamp with Clock

Designers ▪▪ *George and Elaine Knoll and Gladys Smith*

Ever spot a fallen log or a piece of driftwood that captured your eye and imagination? The lamp shown here is a perfect blend of artistry and natural beauty.

What You Need

solid block of wood, preferably aged

lamp parts with ⅜-inch (9 mm) threaded rod, see pages 9-10

harp

finial

light bulb

12 x 12 inch (31 x 31 cm) sheet of cork, ⅛ inch (3 mm) thick

wood glue

battery-operated clock

Danish oil

lamp shade

dried ferns

craft glue

band saw

chain saw

drill with ⅜-inch (9 mm) and 1-inch (2.5 cm) bits

twist bit, 1 x 18 inches (2.5 x 46 cm)

wire brush

belt sander

sandpaper of various grits

craft knife

hand-held rotary tool

What You Do

1. If the wood you've chosen is new and you're in no hurry to make your lamp, place it under cover for several years: rule of thumb is one year of drying for every 2 inches (5 cm) in diameter. Wood that isn't adequately dried will most likely split.

2. Cut the wood block to the size you want for the base, taking care to trim the split ends. Using a chain saw or a band saw, cut the bottom part of the wood square so the lamp will sit level.

3. Drill a ⅜-inch-wide (9 mm) hole, 1 inch (2.5 cm) deep, in the center of the top part of the wood block. In the center of this hole, drill another hole, ½ inch (1.5 cm) wide, through the entire length of the wood block. Now drill your final hole, 1 inch (2.5 cm) wide by 1 inch (2.5 cm) deep, in the bottom of the log where the ½-inch (1.5 cm) hole emerged..

4. Look carefully at the piece of wood and let it tell you whether to cut it, grind it, sand it, polish it—or just leave it alone. Through your own imagination and the wood's natural tendencies, you'll know how far to go in transforming this piece of a tree.

5. After shaping with a band saw or chain saw, the wood is ready to sand. For shaping, start with a 32 grit on a belt sander. Depending on the shape of the surface and what type of equipment is used, you can try various grits, ranging from 50 to 360. A 400 grit is recommended for the final hand sanding. Note: Without a doubt, sanding is the most important part of the entire project. It will make all the difference between a professional and nonprofessional look. Don't forget to wear a good dust mask and follow all safety precautions, including hearing and eye protection.

6. Assemble the lighting components and wire the lamp.

7. To attach feet to the base of the lamp, cut ½ x 1-inch squares (1.5 x 2.5 cm) from a ⅛-inch-thick (3 mm) cork sheet. Glue five to eight squares about ¼ inch (6 mm) from the edge around the bottom of the lamp.

8. Mark where you want the clock to be positioned. Using a hand-held rotary tool, carve out enough wood to house the clock. Insert the clock.

9. Run the lamp cord between the cork feet so you can face the lamp in any direction with the wire running out the back.

10. For an extra smooth finish, hand rub the wood with Danish oil.

11. Glue dried ferns onto the shade.

Lapidary Lamp with Basswood Shade

Designer ▪▪ *Diane Weaver*

This stunning lamp, with its handmade louvered shade, provides you with a luminous stage for showing off your favorite rocks and stones.

What You Need

(13) sheets ⅟₃₂-inch basswood, 3 x 24 inches (8 x 62 cm)

heavyweight black beading thread

20-inch (50 cm) bottom shade fitter ring

5-inch (3 cm) top shade fitter ring with finial and harp connector

(2) 1-inch (2.5 cm) wooden disks, (1) 7½ inches (19 cm) in diameter, (1) 6¼ inches (16 cm) in diameter

(1) ¼-inch (6 mm) wooden disk, 4¾ inches (12.5 cm) in diameter

(2) pieces of ½-inch (1.5 cm) copper pipe, (1) 5 inches long (13 cm), (1) 6½ inches (16.5 cm) long

(2) pieces of ¼-inch copper (1 cm) tubing, 9 inches (23 cm) long

(2) copper tees to fit the tubing at the top of the tee and the ½-inch (1.5 cm) pipe at the base

epoxy for gluing copper

lamp parts with ⅜-inch (9 mm) threaded rod; see pages 9-10

light bulb

harp

finial

plaster impregnated fabric wrap

paper mache pulp

large stones, shells, or other treasures

lightweight colored twine

acrylic paints: black and metallic silver

package of silver composite foil

foil adhesive

(3) rubber bumpers, at least ½ inch (1.5 cm) high

craft knife

(2) sewing needles with large eyes

112

drill with ¼-inch (6 mm) and ⅜-inch
   (9 mm) bits
paintbrushes

What You Do

Making the Shade

1. Use a craft knife to cut out the
shade slats following the pattern (see
figure 1). Four slats can be cut from
each piece of basswood.

2. Drill ¼-inch (6 mm) holes in the
slats, as indicated on the pattern. You
can stack the slats in small piles to
accomplish this task more quickly.

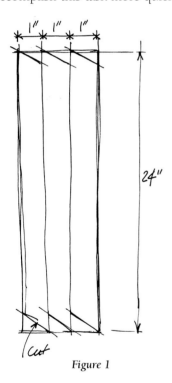

Figure 1

3. Lace the slats to the rings, as
shown in figure 2, working both the
top and the bottom of the slats at the
same time. Placing the rings over a
cardboard cone or lamp shade while
lacing is very helpful.

Making the Base

1. Drill a ⅜-inch (9 mm) hole in the
center of all three wooden disks.

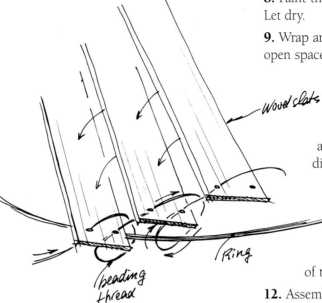

Figure 2

2. Sand the three disks and paint
them black.

3. Form the main section of the lamp
by carefully bending the copper tubing (it kinks easily) to form a relaxed
rectangle. This is most easily done
around a form. A tube bender is helpful, but not essential. You may wish to
run the lamp cord through the copper
sections at this point or feed it
through later with a leader.

4. Use the epoxy to glue the pipes,
connectors, and tubing together, as
shown in figure 3.

5. Wrap the tubing and the tee connectors in the plaster fabric and let
the fabric dry.

6. Apply a 1-inch (2.5 cm) layer of
paper mache all around the rectangle,
smoothing the paper mache as you go.

7. Finish off the joint with a rim of
paper mache at the top of the rectangle and two large stones pressed into
the paper mache at the bottom. Let
it dry.

8. Paint the paper mache rectangle.
Let dry.

9. Wrap and tie the stones in the
open space within the rectangle, using
the colored twine.

10. Apply the foil
adhesive and the silver
foil to the copper pipe
and the largest and smallest
disk, as well as any lamp
parts that will be used
below the bottom rim
of the shade.

11. Glue the rubber
bumpers to the bottom
of the lamp.

12. Assemble and wire the lamp.
Screw in the bulb and attach the
shade and finial.

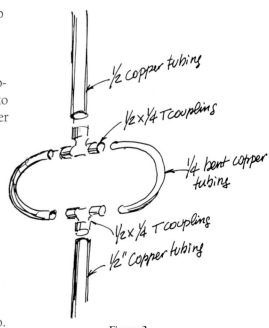

Figure 3

Bamboo Lamp

Designer ▪▪ *Pat Scheible*

Standing tall and serene at five feet, this unusual tripod lamp, with bamboo legs and a Japanese paper shade, has an ethereal and exotic appeal.

What You Need

4 stems of bamboo, each at least 5 feet
(1.5 m) long*
duct tape
package of black polymer clay
quick-drying epoxy
spool of thin-gauge craft wire
water-based glue
floral stem wire
hank of natural raffia
lamp parts; see pages 9-10
compact fluorescent bulb
handmade paper
heavy pruning shears
heavy upholstery needle
*available in the wild, or you can use
bamboo fishing poles

What You Do

1. Make a tripod with three of the four bamboo stems, and secure it temporarily with duct tape.

2. Mold a fat plug of polymer clay around the threaded rod. Set this into the tripod above the cross and press down to mold it around the stems. Then pop it loose and bake, according to the package directions.

3. When cool, set the clay firmly in place above the cross with epoxy, as shown in figure 1.

4. Secure the cross with thin-gauge wire. Then, lash the side rails to the bottom of the tripod with wire. Remove the duct tape. The tripod should now be steady and level.

5. Fold the handmade paper into a pyramid shape (see figure 2) and glue the seam with water-based glue.

6. Shorten the tip of the pyramid until it fits nicely into the upper part of the tripod.

7. Lay a piece of floral wire along the inside of each fold for strength; crimp it to the top of the shade.

8. Thread the upholstery needle with raffia, and secure the shade to the upper tripod by binding the shade to the bamboo legs with a length of raffia.

9. Cover the wire lashings with raffia, as shown in figure 3.

10. Wire the lamp. Screw in the bulb.

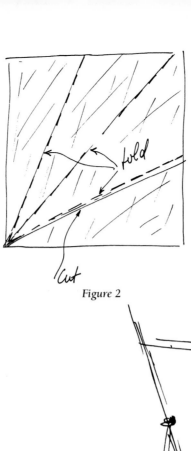

Figure 2

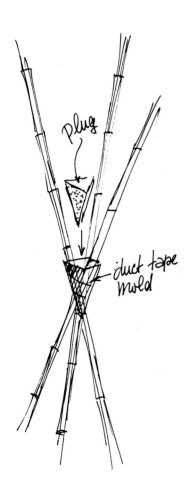

Figure 1

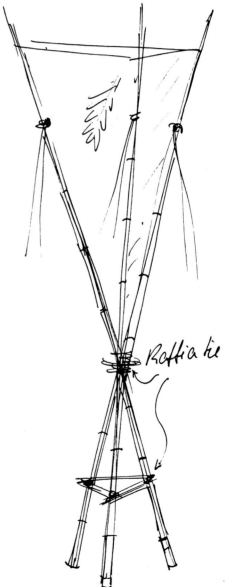

Figure 3

Geode Night Lamp

Designer ▪▪ *Cathy Smith*

As this unusual night light proves, light does wonderful things when it shines through the iridescent colors and striking patterns of geode slices.

What You Need

15 to 18 geode slices of equal thickness, with 5 at least 4 inches (10 cm) tall

rubbing alcohol or witch hazel

waxed paper

paste epoxy compound

craft sticks

plastic Christmas candle

package of black polymer clay

aluminum baking sheet

black acrylic paint

4-watt clear night light bulb

medium-grit sandpaper

sharp ½-inch (1.5 cm) chisel

rolling pin

hacksaw

craft knife

small paintbrush

What You Do

Assembling the Slices

1. Clean the geode slices with rubbing alcohol or witch hazel.

2. Arrange the geode slices on waxed paper so that you have five panels of equal height and width.

3. Mix the epoxy paste. Use a craft stick to apply beads of paste to the spaces between the slices and smooth them down. Use more epoxy to fill in the uneven spaces on the outside of each panel. Note: These panels need to be somewhat (but not perfectly) squared, top and bottom. For the larger slices, use the epoxy to fill in the corners to make an approximate rectangle. Let the epoxy dry; then use the chisel and the sandpaper to clean up the seams.

4. The angle that the panels form is a little over 90 degrees, slightly greater than a right angle. The assembly of the panels is in stages. First, glue together two sets of two panels. Place the two panels side by side on the waxed paper, with their bottoms even and the outside of the panels face down. Next, run a bead of epoxy ¼ to ½ inch (6 mm to 1.5 cm) wide to cover the center 3-inch ((8 cm) seam between the two panels. Allow the epoxy to thicken for 10 to 15 minutes; then stand the panel on its bottom. Carefully fold the panel into a little wider angle than 90 degrees, and brace the outside of the standing panels with two supports (such as two cans of vegetables; this keeps the panels from spreading open and collapsing). Check the outer corner of the panels to make sure the panels are even; adjust their position, if necessary. Gently (keeping the panels in place) smooth the inner bead of epoxy with a craft stick. Don't worry about perfection; after the epoxy cures, it's easily sanded and cleaned up. After the first application of epoxy cures, apply a second bead of epoxy inside and out to finish closing the gaps in the corners. Sand and clean up the seams.

5. Fit together the two double panels and the single panel to form a pentagon. Proceed in stages, applying first a bead of epoxy to hold the structure together, then a second to complete the bond and cover all seams. Most of this will have to be done while the structure is braced in a vertical position. Allow the epoxy seams to cure; sand and clean as before.

Constructing the Base

1. Use a hacksaw to carefully cut the plastic candle down to a height of 1½ inches (4 cm). Cut a little notch in the bottom rim of the candle for the cord so the candle will sit flat. Free up the electrical cord from the rest of the plastic candle.

2. On waxed paper, roll out a circle of polymer clay, about ¼ inch (6 mm) thick and ½ inch (1.5 cm) wider than the geode pentagon.

3. Place the geode structure, bottom down, on top of the clay circle. Press down until the geode bottom rests on the waxed paper. Using the craft knife, trim the clay to fit inside the bottom edge of the geode structure.

4. Lift the geode structure from the clay, and remove any extra clay from the cut out. This is now the base for holding the light fixture. Remember, since all five sides of the pentagon are not symmetrical, the base will fit only one way. Flip the base, bottom side down, onto a baking sheet.

5. Roll and shape the polymer clay to make a cup about ¾ inch (2 cm) high and ⅛ inch (3 mm) thick: this will hold the light fixture. Flare the bottom out with a little extra clay, and cut a notch in the bottom rim of the cup for the electrical cord to pass through. Place the cup on the baking sheet.

6. Bake the base and the cup, according to the package instructions.

7. Paint the light fixture with black acrylic. Don't paint the inside of the socket.

8. After the base is completely cooled, use epoxy to bond the lamp socket to the cup, the cup to the base (align the cup notch with the exit corner for the cord), and the base to the bottom rim of the geode structure. Let the epoxy cure, then clean and sand.

9. Screw in the light bulb.

Plumber's Lamp

Designer ▪▪ *Rich Mathews*

Made from basic plumbing components, this gazellelike lamp can be shaped to assume many graceful forms.

What You Need

precut sections of ½-inch (1.5 cm) and
*   ¾-inch (2 cm) copper piping*
plumbing tees, elbows, and caps
sand
solder
2-4 grommets to fit drilled holes in
*   step 3*
masking tape
aerosol clear lacquer
aerosol flat black or gray paint
lamp parts; see pages 9-10
globe-shaped or thin tubelike bulb
soldering torch
vise
file
drill with ¼-inch (6 m) drill bit
steel wool

What You Do

1. Experiment creating different designs by connecting the individual pieces of pipe with the tees and elbows. Use one central length of pipe for the center, and pivot each additional part to change the form of your lamp. For tall floor lamps, use 1-inch (2.5 cm) diameter piping, and fill the leg pieces with sand to weight the base so it will not tip over. Cap any exposed pipe ends.

2. Secure the pipe to the connecting parts (tees, elbows, caps) with a standard soldering torch. Use just enough solder to solidify the connection, thereby ensuring easier cleanup. File away any excess solder.

3. To shape the socket piece, flatten the top of the central pipe with a vise to create a flat flange. Drill holes in the flange for the socket. You can hide the lamp cord inside the central shaft by drilling a hole approximately 2 inches (5 cm) from the socket and another near the bottom of the central pipe. Line the holes with grommets to prevent wear and tear on the lamp cord.

4. Scrub the pipe sections and connectors with steel wool to brighten the metal.

5. Use tape to mask off the pipe around each elbow and tee; then spray the copper connectors with a clear lacquer. Let dry.

6. Mask the joints, and spray the exposed piping with a flat black or gray paint.

7. Attach the socket, and feed the cord through the central shaft. Screw in the bulb.

Kinetic Lamp with String and Knobs

Designer ▪▪ *Maureen Donahue*

The surface design on this lively lamp is an artful combination of three-dimensional elements and simple painting techniques.

What You Need

(4) pieces of ½ inch (1.5 cm) plywood, 4½ x 11 inches (11 x 28 cm), cut with 45-degree angles on the 11-inch (28 cm) sides

(4) pieces of 1½-inch (4 cm) plywood, 4½ x 4½ inches (11 x 11 cm)

(4) pieces of ¼-inch (6 mm) trim molding, cut to 4½ inches (11 cm) on the short side, with 45-degree angles

wood glue

masking tape

primer

finish sandpaper

2 feet (60 cm) of ¼-inch-wide (6 mm) rope

acrylic paint in teal, purple, black, gold, hot pink, and white

(8) wooden balls or knobs, 1 inch (2.5 cm) in diameter (with a flat spot on one side)

black medium-point paint pen

lamp parts with ⅜-inch (9 mm) threaded rod; see pages 9-10

black lamp shade

harp

finial

light bulb

square

paintbrushes

drill with ⅛-inch (3 mm) and ⅜-inch (9 mm) bits

What You Do

Making the Base

1. Glue together the four pieces of 4½ x 11 x ½ inch (11 x 28 x 1.5 cm) plywood to make an open ended box. Square up the sides and use masking tape to hold the wood square until the glue dries.

2. Glue together the four pieces of 1½ x 4½ x 4½ inch (1.5 x 11 x 11 cm) plywood to form a pyramid.

3. Prime the box, the pyramid, and the four pieces of trim molding, and, when dry, sand well.

Decorating the Base

1. Glue the rope onto the box in swirls and coils. One approach is to trace a bead of glue, then press the rope onto the glue. To hold the rope in place, use small pieces of masking tape, and allow the glue to dry overnight. Be sure to leave room at the bottom of the base for the trim pieces, as well as for the 1-inch (2.5 cm) balls.

2. Remove the tape and paint the base with at least two coats of acrylic paint. Let dry.

3. Dry brush the base with accent colors. To dry brush, simply dip the brush into paint that has been slightly thinned, then wipe the paint off onto a rag. When you dry brush over the raised parts, you will create highlights. Use the hot pink over the purple. Lighten the teal paint with white to

use over the teal. Then use a slight amount of gold here and there.

4. Paint the trim, the pyramid, and the wooden balls.

5. When the paint is dry, glue the trim molding to the box.

6. After the glue dries, lay the box on one side and glue two balls to the side facing up. Let the glue dry for several hours, then glue balls onto another side.

7. Decorate the molding with a paint pen, duplicating the coils and swirls on the lamp base.

Finishing the Lamp

1. Drill a ⅛-inch (3 mm) pilot hole in the top of the pyramid; then drill a ⅜-inch (9 mm) hole.

2. Glue the pyramid to the box with wood glue, being careful not to let any of the glue seep onto the outside of the box.

3. Drill a hole through the back of the box to accommodate the lamp cord.

4. Assemble the lamp components and wire the lamp. Use glue to secure the threaded rod in the hole.

5. Screw in the bulb and attach the shade and finial.

Paper Globe Swag Lamp

Designer ▪▪ Cathy Smith

Hanging paper globes have always been a popular type of lamp, and the distinctive natural fibers in this one add to its radiant allure.

What You Need

3 to 4 yards of ½ inch (1.5 cm) flat reed
2 sheets of banana-mash paper*
round basket hoop, ¾ x 16 inches
    (2 x 40 cm)
2 paper fasteners, 1 inch (2.5 cm) long
white craft glue

acrylic craft paint in white, green, and
    gold
matte acrylic decoupage compound
electrical appliance wire
lighting fixture crossbar, 1 x 4 inches
    (2.5 x 10 cm)

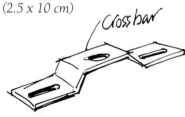

porcelain socket adapter kit
lighting fixture canopy kit with collar
    loop and mounting hardware
swag chain to match hardware
2 wire nuts
light bulb
scissors
craft knife

drill with ⅛-inch (3 mm) bit
small clothespins
old toothbrush
1-inch (2.5 cm) flat paintbrush
measuring tape
blow dryer
tools as indicated in lamp kits

*This is a thin, translucent, naturally brown paper with shreds of banana bark fiber.

What You Do

Making the Lamp

1. Cut four pieces of reed, each 4 feet (1.2 m) long. Stack the strips so the ends are even. Find the center of the strips and drill a ⅛ inch (3 mm) hole straight through the stack, as shown in figure 1.

2. Push the paper fastener through the hole and open the prongs. Spread the strips out to form a star shape. Curl up the ends of one strip and form a circle. Overlap the ends ½ inch (1.5 cm), glue, and clamp, as shown in figure 2. Repeat this process with the other three strips.

3. Hold the connected circle so that the circle's overlapping seams are

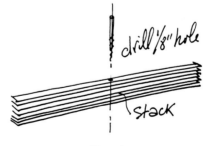

Figure 1

aligned, and drill a ⅛-inch (3 mm) hole through the center of the stacked seams. Push a paper fastener through and open the prongs to hold the strips together.

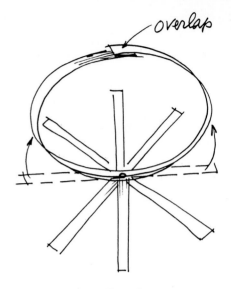

Figure 2

4. Spread the circles out until you have an eight-ribbed ball with ribs equidistant from each other (see figure 3). Glue the intersections together so the ribs can't shift. Use the clothespins to clamp; then let dry.

5. Slide the basket hoop over the top of the ball, as shown in figure 3. Be sure the hoop is level. Glue it in position, clamp, and let dry.

6. Cut two strips from the reed, each 14 inches (35 cm) long. Make two rings from these strips, overlapping the edges ½ inch (1.5 cm); then glue, clamp, and let dry. Make two more

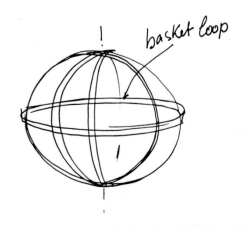

Figure 3

rings that will fit snugly inside these rings and glue them in place. You now have two two-ply hoops, each about 4½ inches (11 cm) in diameter.

7. Center one of these two-ply rings around the top intersection of the ribs on top of the ball, as shown in figure 4. Run a thick bead of glue around the upper rim of the ring, and glue and clamp the ring in place. Wipe off any excess glue and let dry. Repeat this procedure with the other ring for the bottom.

8. Trim the ribs inside of the top and bottom rings, leaving ½-inch (1.5 cm) overhang. Score the reed ribs very

lightly with the craft knife at the inner edge of the rim. Fold the ribs over the rim, as shown in figure 4. Glue and clamp, and allow the reed to dry.

9. Using acrylic paint and an old toothbrush, spatter the three colors of acrylic paint onto the banana paper and let dry.

10. Because the shade is a globe, it's easier to add the paper a half-panel at a time. Cut the paper in a rounded triangle to fit half a panel with a 1-inch (2.5) overhang. Run a bead of glue around the interior of the ribs, hoop, and ring of one panel. Slide the paper (painted side facing out)

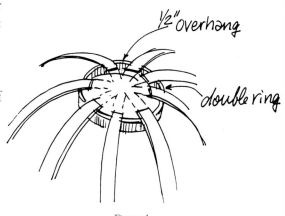

½" overhang

double ring

Figure 4

Paper Globe Swag Lamp

through the frame. Center the panel onto the glued section and gently smooth the paper to the inner edges (see figure 5). Keep the paper surface as taut and unwrinkled as possible. Allow the glue to dry, and trim off excess paper with a sharp blade in the craft knife. Repeat this procedure for the other 15 half-panels. (The last panel is the hardest!)

11. Using the 1-inch (2.5 cm) paintbrush, apply one coat of decoupage compound on the inside of the globe (be sure to coat the edges of the pan-

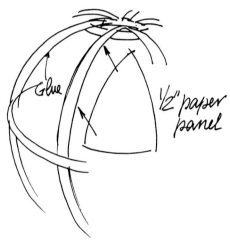

Figure 5

els). Every two to three panels, use the blow dryer on low to dry the paper from the inside. Coat the outside of the globe in the same way, but continue to blow-dry the panels from the inside so the paper will puff out.

12. Cut a length of reed so that you can make a reed coil, ½ inch (1.5 cm) thick, to fit snugly inside the top reed ring, as shown in figure 6. Run a bead of glue along the strip, coil the reed, and glue it in place.

13. Center the lighting fixture crossbar to the underside of the ring, with the hump on the crossbar facing up. Glue it to the underside of the ring and let it dry.

Wiring the Lamp

If you have never wired an appliance to an electrical outlet box, we strongly suggest that you refer to a book on the subject or consult with someone who has this experience.

1. Be sure you cut off the power to the ceiling box before wiring the light to the box.

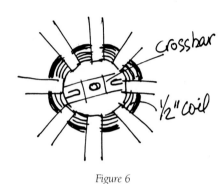

Figure 6

2. Strip off ½ inch (1.5 cm) of insulation from both ends of the appliance wire. Following the instructions on the socket kit, wire the appliance wire to the socket and assemble the socket kit. Don't forget to screw in the light bulb!

3. Insert the threaded nipple with the wire through the center hole on the mounted lighting fixture crossbar, and screw on the collar loop from the canopy kit (see figure 7).

4. Attach the chain to the collar loop and weave the appliance wire through the chain.

5. Assemble the canopy kit, following the manufacturer's directions. Allow an additional 6 inches (15 cm) of appliance wire beyond the canopy for the hookup to the ceiling box. Use wire nuts to connect the lamp to the ceiling box (see figure 7).

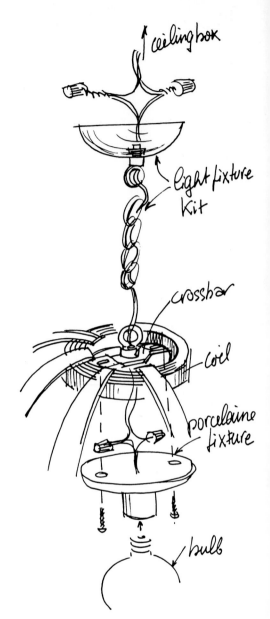

Figure 7

Japanese Washi Lantern

Designer ▪▪ *Mary Ginn*

This extraordinary sculptural lamp, made by wrapping sheets of Japanese paper (*washi*) over a galvanized wire frame, glows with warm light.

What You Need

2 large sheets of Japanese washi paper, approximately 16 x 28 inches (41 x 72 cm). See About Washi on page 126.

large tub, 16 x 28 inches (41 x 72 cm); you can use the kitchen or bath room sink if you have a drying board set up nearby.

drying board*

matte-finish acrylic medium**

3 large clean towels, plus several hand towels

soft tapered brush (a Japanese sumi-e brush works well)

spray bottle and wide-mouth jar of clean water

16-gauge galvanized wire

2 brass-like rings, 4 inches (10 cm) and 7 inches (18 cm) wide

white florist tape

wooden or ceramic base, 8 inches (21 cm) in diameter***

lamp parts with 1-inch (2.5 cm) threaded rod, keyless brass socket, and 8-foot (2.4 m) brown lamp cord; see pages 9-10

low-watt bulb

wire-cutting pliers

*You can make yours with a 4 x 8 foot (1.2 x 2.4 m) piece of drywall, ½ inch (1.5 cm) thick, cut in half crosswise, (or

Japanese Washi Lantern

use scrap pieces of drywall). Finish the edges with duct tape. A weathered piece of plywood also works, but avoid new plywood because it will discolor the paper.

** Available in art-supply stores

***The lamp base shown here is a hand-thrown ceramic piece. You can purchase a flat, round wooden base at craft-supply stores, and oil or paint it to produce the effect you like.

What You Do

About Washi

Renowned for its strength, longevity, and beauty, washi is a Japanese paper often used in museums for restoration of art work, books, and manuscripts. Originating from the bark of the kozo tree, gampi, or mitsumata plants, the paper requires a labor-intensive process done completely by hand, eliminating the need for chemical additives. The result is a strong, fibrous paper with a delicate translucence.

These instructions are geared toward using purchased paper. If you want to tackle making your own washi paper, be sure to work with it fresh. Older paper is not as flexible and doesn't respond as well to complex shapes. A good resource is Timothy Barrett's *Japanese Papermaking/Traditions, Tools, and Techniques*, published by Weatherhill. You can also check the library or Internet for other references.

Soaking the Paper

1. Set up two tables in an L-shape. One will serve as the lampmaking surface and the other will hold the paper-soaking tub. Place one large towel on the lampmaking surface and one on the tub table.

2. Fill the tub with about 4 inches (10 cm) of water.

3. Prop the drying board at about a 60-degree angle against the work surface table, with one of the drying towels (folded several times) underneath the bottom edge. This soaks up any excess water.

4. Place the Japanese paper in the tub and soak it for at least two hours. Don't worry that it will fall apart: the tightly woven fibers have a remarkable resiliency. If the paper is too big for the tub, dip it in the water at midpoint and rip the sheet in half crosswise *with* the grain. Note: Always rip with the grain so you'll get an even, feathery tear. If you're having trouble tearing it, draw a line on the wet paper with a ruler, then rip. Never cut the paper. Cutting reduces the paper's ability to feather onto itself—an essential element in making this lamp.

Building the Wire Frame

1. While the paper soaks, cut eight 14-inch-long pieces of (36 cm) wire. Since this wire usually comes wound in a loose circle, don't straighten it. Your cut pieces of wire will then have a nice curve to them.

2. Gather the wires in a bunch and flatten them out in your hand, bending them once on the edge of the table against the curve so that the curves are identical. This will give you a double curve resembling a capital "B."

3. Starting with the 7-inch (18 cm) brass ring, which will serve as the bottom of your lamp, attach the wire at equal intervals around the ring. Make sure the roundness of the curves faces outward. You do this by wrapping the $1/2$-inch (1.5 cm) end of the wire two or three times around the brass ring with pliers, keeping it tightly wound. Then crimp the wire. It might help in

the spacing process to visually divide the ring into fourths, wrapping those wires first. Then finish off in eighths with the last four wires. This part of the project takes practice and a certain finesse, so don't give up.

4. After all the wires are attached at equal intervals, use about 3 inches (8 cm) of the white florist tape to wrap each joint and the brass ring all the way around. This gives a nice clean surface on which to wrap the paper.

5. As in step 3, attach the opposite end of the wire to the 4-inch (10 cm) brass ring at the top of the lamp. Push gently on the entire frame to make sure it's symmetrical. Finish off the top joints of the ring with florist tape the same way you wrapped the bottom ring.

6. There's no need to wrap the remainder of the frame. You're now ready to cover it with washi.

Wrapping the Wire Frame

1. Lift the paper out of the water and press it gently onto the drying board. It should be completely flat with no pockets of air underneath the surface. As you work the paper, periodically spray it with water to keep it soft and flexible.

2. You will be alternating panels in order to cover the wire on the inside of the lamp. Start the first panel by ripping a strip of paper with the grain, crosswise, that is wide enough to allow about a $1/2$-inch (1.5 cm) feathered edge. This edge should go past the width of the wire section completely around the strip.

3. With the lamp frame on its side (you can prop each end with a rolled hand towel), lay the wet strip over the first wire section, gently pulling it flat.

4. Using a very wet brush and short,

gentle strokes, brush the paper against the wire to tack it in place. Then work the paper over the wire with your fingers so that the paper adheres to itself on the underside of the panel.

5. Feather the paper onto itself with a wet brush. Keeping the brush soaked prevents the paper from pulling and ripping. The water also helps in weaving the fibers together and strengthening the paper.

6. Your first completed panel should look taut, smooth, and slightly concave. Do the same on every other section, ending with a total of four alternating covered panels. Spray the panels with water at intervals to keep the surfaces wet while you work.

7. To complete the last four panels, rip the strips the same size as the previous four, and place them so they overlap the paper panels attached to the lamp on either side.

8. Using a fully soaked brush again, feather the paper onto itself. Then work it with your fingers over the top and bottom edges, feathering it with the brush on the underside.

9. Set the lamp upright to dry. It will tighten to the frame as it dries.

10. On the dry paper, lightly brush all seams, inside and out, with the acrylic medium, concentrating on the feathered edges. This medium will hold the seams together and won't discolor over time. There will be a slight difference in the surface quality where you have applied the medium. If this bothers you, you can brush it all over the lamp.

11. Wire the base and screw in the bulb.

12. Position the dry shade on the circular base.

Arts and Crafts Lamp

Designer ▪▪ *Rich Mathews*

This handsome lamp captures the simple and timeless elegance of woodworking created during the popular Arts and Crafts movement.

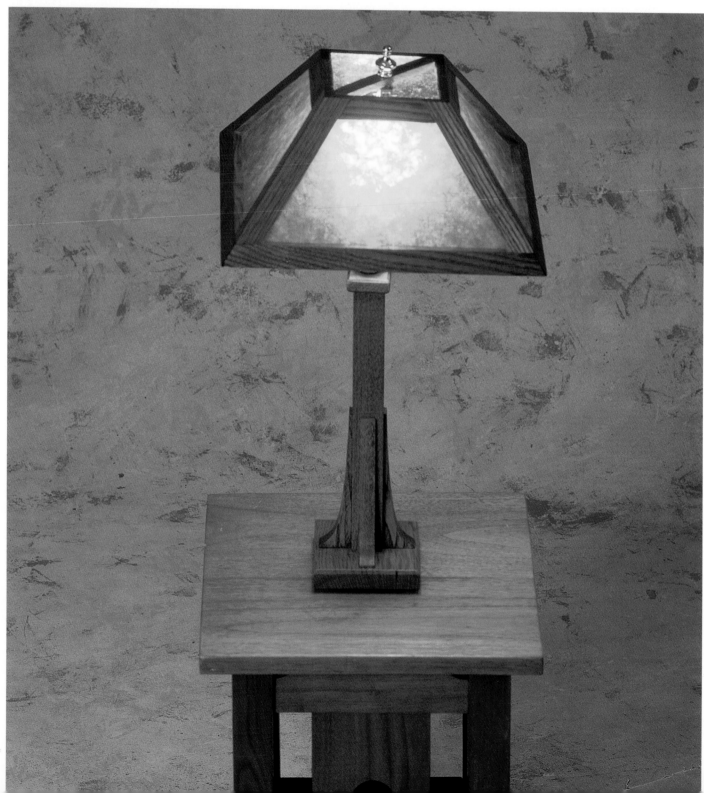

Cut List

12-14 feet (3-4 m) of oak strips, ⅜ inch thick x 1 inch wide (9 mm x 2.5 cm)

(1) ¾-inch (2 cm) oak base, 4½ x 4½ inches (11 x 11 cm)

1¼ x 12-inch (3.2 x 30.5 cm) oak shaft

(4) oak foot brackets, ¾-inch (2 cm) wide

(1) oak cap, 1¾ x ¾ inch (4 x 2 cm)

What You Need

oak-colored wood stain

disposable latex gloves

quick-drying epoxy

sheets of mica panel*

clear acrylic varnish

lamp parts; see pages 9-10

clip-on top shade fitter ring, or clip-on adapted for use with a finial

felt or plastic "feet" for the base

table saw with a rip fence

sandpaper

paintbrushes

framing square

straightedge

utility knife with several sharp blades

miter box or tenon saw

clamps

router (optional)

drill with assorted bits

*Available from mail-order suppliers in 24 x 30-inch (60 cm x 75 cm) sheets

What You Do

Making the Shade

1. Cut a bevel along one edge of all your ⅜-inch (9 mm) oak strips using a table saw with a rip fence. *Use a push strip!* These are thin strips of wood you're ripping (see figure 1).

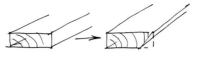

Figure 1

Note: The splay of the shade is determined by the angle of the bevel you cut. Your angle must be between 45 and 90 degrees. The closer to the vertical you set your saw blade, the more splayed out your shade will be.

2. Once you've determined the angle of your bevel and ripped your stock, cut the eight pieces you need for the four corner edges. Cut them all to the same length, making them a couple of inches longer than your final goal, because you'll be trimming them off midway through the process.

3. Sand the oak strips well, then stain them and let dry.

4. Mix up enough quick-drying epoxy to edge-glue one pair of corner pieces, as shown in figure 2. Put on a pair of

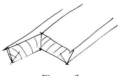

Figure 2

latex gloves and brush glue on the bevel surface of both pieces. There are at least 93 different ways to try to clamp these together but, unless you're Norm Abrams, just about every one of them will fail. So, forget about proving how great a craftsperson you are. Just hold the two pieces clamped tightly in your gloved hands until the epoxy sets up. Turn on the radio or television first and just relax!

5. Repeat this gluing-up process three more times to get all four edge corners assembled.

6. Now it's time to figure out the shape of the four-panel mica. You're

going to cut a trapezoid-shaped piece. The first step is to determine the angle of the side. There's a mathematical way to do this, but the following approach works great.

a. As shown in figure 3, lay your framing square flat on a table with the corner out over the edge, far enough out to create a triangle of open space between the inside corner of the

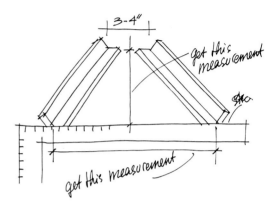

square and the edge of the table. Next, insert your edge assembly in this triangle and tilt it over the table until both sides can be snugged up against the inside edges of the framing square. When this happens, you've got the correct angle for your edge assembly. Scribe a line in the wood along the edge of the framing square to indicate where to cut.

b. Set your table saw blade to this angle and crosscut to your scribed line. Make a parallel cut at the other end of the edge assembly. Cut the three edge assemblies the same way.

c. Now, lay a straightedge on your bench and place two edge assemblies opposite each other on your bench, with the ends sitting flat up against the edge, as shown in figure 3. If you made the cuts correctly, these should be the opposing sides of your trapezoid. Move them together or apart until the top ends are 3 to 4 inches (8-10 cm) apart. Now you can measure the base.

Arts and Crafts Lamp

7. Now you can use these measurements to cut out your mica. Set the angle of your table saw so you can crosscut the proper angle on the top and bottom of your edge assemblies.

8. Next, decide on the narrow dimension at the top of the trapezoid; 3 to 4 inches (8-10 cm) usually works well. This means that, when all four sides are assembled, there will be a 3- to 4-inch (8-10 cm) square opening at the top.

9. Make the top and side cuts in the mica sheet with a utility knife and a straightedge. (You'll need to make several passes with the knife and change the blade quite often.)

10. Lay the piece of mica into one pair of your edge assemblies, and mark where the bottom edge needs to be cut. Make the cut, check the fit, and cut three more just like it (see figure 4).

11. Glue one sheet of mica to the inside of one pair of edge assemblies. Then glue another into the other pair. Stand those two pieces up parallel to each other, resting on the edge assemblies, and glue the third sheet in place. Then, glue the last piece in place.

12. Now you need to cut and fit the top and bottom rails in place. This is all eyeball stuff, no measuring. Hold the strip up against the edge assemblies where it's supposed to fit, scribe your lines, and then cut to your line. You can do this with your table saw, a miter box, or a tenon saw. Once each piece fits, glue it into place, and clamp until the glue dries.

13. If everything went well, you now have a truncated pyramid. All that remains is to fit a small nonbevel strip in the center of the top opening to support the shade on your lamp assembly, as shown in figure 5.

14. Apply a coat of varnish to the wood and let dry.

Making the Stand

1. Using a table saw, bevel the upper edges of the 4½-inch-square (11 x 11 cm) oak base.

2. Drill a hole through the center of the base, making it large enough to accommodate the threaded rod .

3. Drill a similar hole through the center of the oak cap.

4. To prepare the shaft for the threaded rod, first use a table saw to cut the shaft in half along its length. Next, with your table saw or a router, cut a centered groove down the length of each half. (These grooves must be wide enough to accommodate the threaded rod.) Glue the two halves of the shaft back together with a quick-drying epoxy.

5. Sand and stain all the oak pieces for the stand.

6. Glue one end of the shaft to the base, centering the holes as you do. Then clamp the pieces together until the glue has dried. Also glue the cap to the top of shaft, carefully centering the holes. Finally, glue the four feet to the bottom of the base. (The feet will "lift" the base so that the lamp cord has room to exit from the bottom of the lamp stand.)

7. Glue the four foot brackets to the base, centering them on the four flat surfaces of the shaft.

8. When the glue has dried, insert the threaded rod down through the hole in the lamp-stand assembly. Then tighten a threaded nut onto each end of the tube to hold it in place.

9. Wire the stand. Screw in the light bulb and clip on the shade.

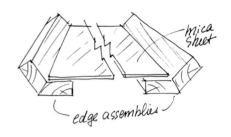

Figure 4

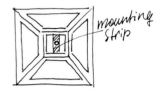

Figure 5

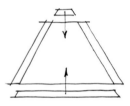

Figure 6

Reading Lamp No 1., from How to Make Mission Style Lamps and Shades *(**Popular Mechanics Co.**, 1911)*

Contributing Designers

Maureen (Cha Cha) Donahue is a graphic artist who lives and works in Asheville, North Carolina. She has always been very creative, and makes all types of craft projects.

Sheila Ennis-Schulz is a former freelance writer, who now makes her living in Boston, Massachusetts as a decorative paint finisher. She specializes in walls, cabinetry, and furniture, applying her enthusiasm for crafts to anything that involves paints. Designing lamps with great visual appeal is a natural off-shoot of her current business.

Mary Ginn, through her company Firefly Design, makes and markets unique and beautiful lamps, using traditional Japanese paper, called washi, sculptural wire frames, and hand-thrown ceramic bases. You can visit her website, homepage home1.gte.net/bginn/index.htm, or write: Firefly Design, 20415 80th N.E., Bothell, WA 98011

Bobby Hansson has been making sculpture, furniture, and musical instruments from found objects since 1955. A former professional photographer, he now operates the Leaping Beaver Tinker Shop in Rising Sun, Maryland, and specializes in working with recycled objects. He is the author of The Fine Art of the Tin Can (Lark Books, 1996).

Margaret (Peggy) Hayes creates custom painted furniture and cross-stitch designs. She credits much of her inspiration to her husband of 24 years, Charles. They live in Fletcher, North Carolina.

Dana Irwin is a graphic artist and watercolor painter who lives in Asheville, North Carolina, with two dogs and two cats. She began working with lamps as a teenager in her father's plating company, where she often salvaged brass lamps from auction sales, and has been a lamp lover and collector ever since.

George Knoll has been making high-quality and innovative products for the home and office since 1989, using fallen hardwoods from the mountains of Western North Carolina. Elaine Knoll and Gladys Smith make a variety of craft items, including the lamp shades on George's lamps. Write to Green Valley Wood Crafts, PO Box 398, Leicester, NC 28748, or send e-mail to gfknoll@aolcom.

Shelley Lowell owns Pink Neck Gallery, an art gallery, in Asheville, North Carolina. A painter, sculptor, illustrator, and graphic designer, she received her BFA at Pratt Institute in New York, and now teaches a variety of art classes, including hand-painted furniture, in the Asheville area. .

Rich Mathews is an avid fan of Arts and Crafts-style objects. Being a handyman of sorts, he has tried his hand at making some lamps, tables, and mirrors in recent years that echo the spirit of that era. Most of them, being flawed in one way or another, are best labeled "prototypes," but he gets to see the "real thing" every year at the Arts and Crafts conference held every year in Asheville, North Carolina. In real life, he drives a desk in Western North Carolina and works on several community networking initiatives.

Nancy McGaha feels that living in the mountains of Western North Carolina has enhanced her creative spirit. She enjoys working in a variety of media, including beads, smocking, weaving, fiber arts, and any combination of these.

Jim Muesing designs and markets a line of one-of-a-kind lamps made from old books, using high-quality brass fittings. He lives and works in Asheville, North Carolina.

Olivier Rollin is a French multimedia artist, formally trained in industrial design, who now resides in Asheville, North Carolina.

Karyn Sanders makes one-of-a-kind wedding gowns, christening gowns, and accessories for private clients. Her work has appeared in Victoria and McCalls magazines. She sells silk ribbon kits through her mail-order business, Sweet Material Things, in Walkill, New York.

Pat Scheible keeps busy with trompe l'oeil and faux finish work for commercial and residential clients in the southeast. Creative and zany ideas spill over into painted furniture, birdhouses, and lamps. She lives in Mebane, North Carolina.

M.C. (Cathy) Smith is an artist who works in a variety of media. She is currently following her destiny in western North Carolina, accompanied and encouraged in this pursuit by husband, son, and assorted feline, canine and reptilian family members.

Mark Strom is a professional wood sculptor whose work covers a broad range of applications. During the last three years, he has focused on liturgical sculpture, commissioned by churches throughout the Southeast. He is co-owner of Loth Lorien Woodworking, in Asheville, North Carolina.

Ginger Summit, co-author of The Complete Book of Gourd Crafts (Lark Books, 1996) and author of Gourds in Your Garden (Hillway Press, 1998), has been fascinated by gourds ever since she retired from teaching seven years ago. She feels passionate about gourds and derives great pleasure from working with them. She lives in Los Altos Hills, California, with her husband, Roger, and is currently working on her next book, a guide to making gourd musical instruments.

Terry Taylor is an artist whose work takes many forms, including the pique-assiette technique for making mosaics, beadwork, and one-of-a-kind cards. He lives in Asheville, North Carolina.

Diane Weaver is the author of Painted Furniture (Sterling/Lark, 1995). She received her Bachelor of Fine Arts from Wayne State University in Michigan, and now spends her days painting in Fairview, North Carolina, where she lives with her husband, Dick, and their dog, Rosie.

David Williamson is a professor of art at Baldwin-Wallace College in Berea, Ohio, where he has taught for 22 years. Working on lamps is more than a hobby for him—it is an art form. While his artistic expression in the medium of found objects has taken different forms, lamps have been a recurring theme in his work over the past 20 years.

Pamella (Wil) Wilson is an accomplished potter and visual artist who has lived in Asheville, North Carolina for ten years, and claims a deep love for both the mountains and the ocean. Wil currently works as kit manager for the Lark Books catalogue.

Ellen Zahorec is a mixed-media studio artist, specializing in handmade paper and collage. Her work has been shown internationally and is part of numerous private and corporate collections. She lives in Cincinatti, Ohio.

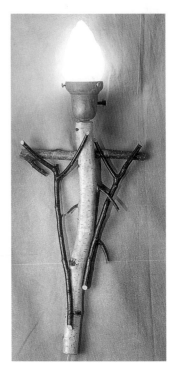

RICK MELBY
St. Sebastian's
Nightlight, 1995
18" x 15" x 7" (45
x 37.50 x 17.5 cm)
Recycled materials:
stainless steel
screen, copper
cloth, etched glass
rods, slate
PHOTO BY CHRIS COXWELL

JERRY WOMACKS
Globe Sconce, 1994
23" x 9" (57.5 x 22.5 cm)
Birch wood, glass globe, brass
PHOTO BY JERRY ANTHONY

GARRY KNOX BENNETT
Windmill and Arrow, 1996
17" x 10" x 8-1/2" (42.5 x
25 x 21 cm)
Painted wood
PHOTO BY F. LEE FATHEREE

Far right
CHRIS DARWAY
Wedgie Lamp, 1994
12" x 6" x 7" (30 x 15
x 17.5 cm)
Copper, aluminum,
brass, bronze, cast resin
PHOTO BY CHET BOLINS

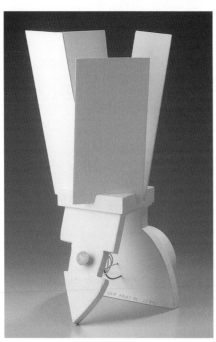